What's Inside:

This book will show you how to be a hypnotist in less than an hour, to perform for your friends and family, and to do astounding feats of mind control that will make you the envy of everyone.

Beyond that, hypnosis – as you're about to discover – can awaken the power of your subconscious mind to break through self-limitations to help you achieve your personal performance goals.

Ready? Let's Begin!

Fun With Hypnosis

BY PROFESSOR SVENGALI

International Standard Book Number 0-9663985-0-5
Library of Congress Catalog Card Number 98-091470
Printed in the United States of America
Published by Phat Publishing.
David M. Geliebter, Publisher
319 Algonquin Road, Franklin Lakes, NJ 07417

Table of Contents

PREFACE   I

C H A P T E R   1
AN INTRODUCTION TO HYPNOSIS

Modern Hypnosis Starts With Mesmer   3

Mesmerism Attracts King Louis   4
XVI & Marie Antoinette

Braid Coins "Hypnosis"   4

Freud Enters The Picture   4

Coue' Authors Autosuggestion   5

As Scientific Interest Fades,   6
The Hucksters Appear

World War II Brings The Medical   6
Community Back

Erickson Hypnotized With A Handshake   6

C H A P T E R   2
REMOVING THE MYSTERY BEHIND
HYPNOSIS

"Look Into My Eyes..."   8

We All Encounter Hypnosis Daily   8

What Hypnosis Feels Like   9

How Hypnosis Works   9

Hypnosis is The Opposite of Sleep   9

Habits Hold The Key To Hypnosis   10

Hypnosis Is A Matter Of Suggestibility   11

Mozart Knew How To Tap His   11
Subconscious

Enstein Did, Too   11

How Genius Works   12

Conscious vs. Subconscious Mind   12

Einstein Put His Intuitive Abilities To Work.   12

Can We All Be Mozarts and Einsteins?   13

You Are The Bus Driver On The Road To   13
The Subconscious Mind

Are You Left Or Right Brain? An Easy Test   14

C H A P T E R   3
TESTING

Testing Identifies Suggestibility   15

Confidence Is Key   15

How To Start Out   16

The "Hand Drop" Test   16

The "Pendulum Swing" Test   17

The "Hands Up" Test   18

The "Magic Hands" Test   19

The "Falling Forwards - Falling Backwards" Test   20

The "Hands Together" Test   22

Some Concluding Thoughts   23

Five Rules of Testing   24

C H A P T E R   4
INDUCING A TRANCE

The "Eye Fixation" Method   25

The "Arm Levitation" Method   31

Two "Rapid Induction" Techniques   35

The "Eye-To-Eye" Method   35

The "Special Nerve" Method   37

Ten Rules of Induction   38

A Footnote To Induction   39

CHAPTER 5
DEEPENING TECHNIQUES

Rigid Arm   41

The Staircase   42

Head Down   43

Awaken And Go Deeper   43

Forget Your Name   45

The Five Rules of Deepening   46

CHAPTER 6
HYPNOTIC ROUTINES

Stuck Like Glue   48

Magic X-Ray Vision   51

Who Nose What Turns You On   53

A Half Dozen More Hypnotic Routines   55
- Fingers Stuck
- Shaky Hands
- Fingers in The Ears
- So You Want To Be in Shoe Business?
- So You Think You're Strong, Huh?
- A Penny For Your Thoughts

The Five Rules of Suggestion   56

CHAPTER 7
OTHER SENSATIONAL STUFF YOU CAN DO

The "Lemon Aid" Illusion   58

Water To Whiskey   58

The Invisible Man   59

Bunny Love   59

Age Regression   60

Ten More Sensational Hypnotic Routines   62
- The Virgin and The Tramp
- Rock-A-By-Baby
- Magnetic Powers
- You Can't Do it
- You're Getting Sleepy
- Rubber Nose
- Is Anything Wrong
- A Hot Date Tonight
- Shower Power
- Tennis Anyone?

CHAPTER 8
STAGE HYPNOSIS

The Opening Lecture   66

Waking Suggestions: The Lemon Test   67

Hand Magic   68

Invitation on Stage   69

Open Eye Test   70

The Arm Stretch Test   71

The Main Performance   71

The Deepening Phase   72

An Alternate: Instant Hypnosis   76

The Routine   76

The Domino Effect   77

The More The Merrier   78

X-Ray Vision   78

Saturday Matinee   79

Fountain of Youth   80

Attack of Amnesia   82

Trip To Pluto   85

Three-Ring Circus   87

Two Great Finales   88
- The Human Bridge
- The Ring of Fire

The Finish   92

A Couple of Afterthoughts   92

Ten More Stage Rouitines   93
- Madonna
- Give Me a Hug
- Male Stripper
- The Waiter
- Who Wears The Pants in The Family
- Make Up Your Mind
- Roses Are Red
- Catch Any Fish Lately
- The Hindu Rope Routine

Stage Preparation   97

Ten Rules of Stage Hypnotism   97

CHAPTER 9
SELF-HYPNOSIS

The Preparation Phase   99

Script For The Long Method of Induction   99

Smoking Conditioning   102

Dieting Conditioning   103

Drinking Conditioning   103

Pain Control Conditioning   104

The Awakening Process   105

Self-Hypnosis, The Short Version   108

Rapid Self-Hypnosis Conditioning Statements   109

The Five Rules of Self-Hypnosis   110

CHAPTER 10
ODDS & ENDS

The Power of the Mind   109

Five Pathways to Greatness   110
- Use Your Whole Brain
- Think Positive Thoughts, Imagine Success
- Relax Your Brain
- Set Success Goals
- Failure is Only For Losers

Some Final Words of Wisdom   112

In Conclusion   112

BIBLIOGRAPHY   113

ABOUT THE AUTHOR   114

NOTES   115

A Few Words About The World of Hypnosis

Get ready to amaze your friends - and amaze yourself - with your new-found powers of hypnosis.

ou're about to enter the world of hypnosis, a thoroughly fascinating world filled with both wonder and delight. It's like nothing else you'll ever experience!

There seems to be this aura of mystery surrounding hypnotism: how it really works, and what the forbidden secrets are that hold the key to its amazing powers. I'm about to explode any myths about ancient secrets or special knowledge needed. *There aren't any*. Hypnosis is a natural science, and the application of its power is simple to learn.

This book will show you how to be a hypnotist in less than an hour, how to perform for your friends and family, and to do astounding feats of mind control that will make you the envy of everyone.

Beyond that, hypnosis – as you're about to discover -- can awaken the power of your subconscious mind to break through self-limitations, to help you achieve your personal performance goals.

I first became curious about this subject while visiting Las Vegas. A stage hypnotist was performing an afternoon show at our hotel and I thought it would be an interesting diversion from the sun and gaming tables. What I didn't expect was to be so drawn into what was taking place on stage. A dozen people, all strangers, being instantly transformed into willing subjects. And all too willing they were. Whatever he said, they did.

The hypnotist told one young lady she was Madonna, and the next thing you know she's strutting her stuff on stage, lip-syncing to the voice of the famous singer. Another man was told he was totally naked, but that his manhood was huge! He had a grin from ear-to-ear. When the hypnotist told him his pride and joy had shrunk down to the size of a raisin, he immediately covered up from embarrassment and hid behind a chair. So it went for almost two hours straight. One person was told he was from outer space, another became a human bridge, and on and on. It was a circus of performers, except they were people who only minutes earlier were audience members, like me. I was in total awe.

At first it was curiosity that drew me in. Then, after it completely hit me a few days later, I was frightened. How could this person have so much control over these people? How could these apparently sensible people have so easily succumbed to his charms? I had to know the answers. When I got back to New York, I ran to the library to find out everything I could about hypnosis.

There wasn't much apart from the clinical primers and psychology textbooks, which were way over my head. Magic shops carried a few books on stage hypnotism, but they were written some 50 years ago.

Fortunately I discovered a school, The American School of Hypnosis. I couldn't wait. I enrolled right over the phone. Upon being graduated, certificate in hand, I rushed out to find my first hypnosis subject. While I acted like an old pro, I was really nervous. Could I do it? Did I have the skills? I did! She was under my spell in no time. Wow, was it a great feeling! It still is. What was equally amazing was how simple it was to be a hypnotist, once you know how.

For too long I've said I wished someone would make a simple-to-read-and-understand book on how hypnosis works, the definitive *"how-to"* on this subject: a book that would tell you everything you needed to be the consummate hypnotist; a book that, step-by-step, with word-for-word scripts, would impart every trick-of-the-trade and bit of wisdom needed to perform like a pro. *This book is the result.*

I'm pleased to be able to share it all with you. Study the lessons well and you'll be hypnotizing people before you know it!

Good luck and have fun,

PROFESSOR SVENGALI

PS   To make the reading simpler, the author has chosen to use "he" (or the generic "subject") when making reference to an individual, whether male or female.

Chapter

An Introduction To Hypnosis

"Men are not prisoners of fate, only prisoners of their own minds." Franklin D. Roosevelt.

References to early accounts of the hypnotic phenomena can be found in such sources as the Bible and the Talmud. Some might even argue that Adam and Eve were hypnotized into eating the forbidden fruit, mesmerized by the animal magnetism of their Garden of Eden serpent friend.

Descriptions of trance states and healing miracles are legend among Greek oracles, Persian magi, Hindu fakirs, and Indian yogi. Similarly, miraculous cures attributed for centuries to the "royal touch" of kings and princes, as well as the astonishing achievements of faith healers, may all be viewed as having a basis in hypnotic suggestion.

Modern Hypnosis Starts With Mesmer

Modern hypnosis had its beginnings some two hundred years ago. In the eighteenth century Franz Mesmer (from which the word "mesmerized" comes), an Austrian physician, conjectured that the root of hypnosis lay in a magnetic fluid that flowed inside all living creatures. His claims of "animal magnetism" were not widely accepted by his Viennese colleagues, so in 1778, he left for Paris. There he practiced such theatrics as bringing together groups of patients on stage for live sessions. These assemblies involved the use of a large oak tub filled with water, iron filings, and powered glass. Patients placed their bodies against iron rods protruding from the tub.

Mesmer would appear on stage in a long flowing silk robe, and accompanied by piano music, make passes over the patients with a long iron rod, attempting to draw out any "bad" fluids. Amazingly, most people were cured in only a few sessions. Unable to formulate any convincing scientific explanation, he was once again denounced as a quack by his peers.

Mesmerism Attracts King Louis XVI and Marie Antoinette

Nevertheless "mesmerism," as it was called then, had gained many important disciples including France's Queen Marie Antoinette and King Louis XVI. Mesmer's home and office never contained less than two hundred patients, constantly coming and going.

In 1784, the King appointed a royal commission to investigate and test mesmeric treatment. Benjamin Franklin, who at the time was serving as U.S. Ambassador to France, along with the physician Joseph Guillotine (better known for the killing instrument he invented), after much inquiry agreed that some patients were indeed cured, yet no absolute link could be established to Mesmer's theories of a universal magnetic fluid that could be transferred from him to inanimate objects and then to his patients. Their final conclusions rested on the thesis that, "The excitement of the *imagination* is the true cause of the effects."

Braid Coins "Hypnosis"

In the nineteenth century, James Braid, a Scottish surgeon, through his observations, coined the word "neurohypnotism," or nervous sleep (from the Greek *hypno*, or "to sleep"), later shortened to just "hypnosis." Braid was initially so skeptical about the claims of mesmerism that in 1841 he tried to expose it as fake during a public demonstration by a touring mesmerist. Instead, he became convinced that the girl on stage was indeed in a genuine trance. His investigations eventually lead him to conclude that hypnotic phenomena is the result of suggestion, and the power of hypnosis, the power of mind over body, resides in all of us.

All this was occurring before the days of modern drugs for surgery and pain treatment. It's no wonder, then, that hypnosis was embraced among the medical community as a valid anesthesia during surgery and as having curative powers over aches and pains. British surgeon James Esdaile, in the span of two years, performed over 3,000 operations, including amputations, cataract removals, and tumor removals, using the mesmeric process of inducing anesthesia. Not only were his patients insensitive to pain, their post surgery recovery rate was significantly higher.

Freud Enters The Picture

Many noted scientists researched the hypnosis phenomena, among them, Sigmund Freud. Freud, who was introduced to the subject by a stage hypnotist, spent a number of years studying the subject, fueled by his interest in the cause of neurosis, sighting, "There could be powerful mental processes which nevertheless remain hidden from the consciousness of men."

Freud was not what you would call the best hypnotist in the world, to be kind. He also became quite frustrated when patients resisted opening up under hypnosis. It was then that he began to use more active measures, placing his hands directly on the patient's head and loudly and forcefully stating, "Through the pressure of my hands it will come to the mind." With this method, Freud was able to produce results similar to those gained under hypnosis.

A short time later he introduced his now famous psychoanalytic couch routine, where a patient is asked to lie down, relax, and freely associate about his problems. Thus was born the *age of psychoanalysis.*

Freud's initial rejection of hypnosis as a legitimate therapeutic method was later modified after he experienced its usefulness in the treatment of war neurosis in soldiers following World War I. His early rebuff was a definite deterrent to others, and interest among the medical and scientific world waned significantly.

Two exceptions were a couple of Frenchmen, Pierre Janet, a noted neurologist and psychologist, and Emile Coue', who went on to open the "new Nancy school." Janet originally opposed the use of hypnosis but quickly became one of its biggest advocates after he discovered its relaxing effects and usefulness in promoting healing. He postulated that there were multiple layers of consciousness and hidden underlying causes for manifest pathological symptoms.

Coue' Authors Autosuggestion

Coue' was the modern-day author of the idea of *autosuggestion.* Where in hypnosis the suggestions are given in the *subconscious* state, Coue' insisted his patients give themselves suggestions while fully *conscious.*

His insights into the mystery behind the curative powers of hypnosis went unnoticed at the time. Coue' denied the discovery of autosuggestion to be his, instead giving credit to the likes of Aristotle, who taught that, "A vivid imagination compels the body to obey it," and Saint Thomas Aquinas, who stated, "Every idea conceived by the mind is an order which the organism obeys." Coue's conclusions were that it is impossible to separate the physical from the mental, the body from the mind. Not only are they dependent on one another, they are really one.

As Scientific Interest Fades, The Hucksters Appear

By the latter part of the 1800s and the early part of this century, with research into the matter still inconclusive, psychoanalysis all the rage, and with the discovery of chloroform, ether and "modern drugs" like aspirin in wide use, scientific interest in hypnosis faded, only to be renewed by the public and their interest in the strange and unusual.

This was, after all, the period of P.T. Barnum, the traveling tent show, and amazing circus attractions like the bearded woman and Tiny Tim, an era of exploitation, or huckterism, of *a sucker born every minute.* It was a perfect atmosphere for hypnosis to be inhaled into to the whirlwind of excitement surrounding anything sensational and thrilling. And it was. Many people were fascinated. Many, of course, thought it to be shameless exploitation.

Traveling hypnotists, capitalizing on this huge appetite the public had for the extraordinary, performed in everything from fancy, black-tie night clubs, to raudy concert halls, to smoke-filled beer joints and speakeasies. Most were legitimate performers. Hypnotists were the equivalent of today's touring rock and roll bands. And yes, hypnotism had its Milli Vanilli, too. Some were fakes who used conspirators planted in the audience. After a while, though, like vaudeville, hypnosis faded from view.

World War II Brings The Medical Community Back

A renewed interest came about after World War II, as practitioners in the fields of medicine, dentistry, and psychology all showed interest in applying the techniques of hypnosis. By the 1950s, the American and British medical associations validated hypnosis as a legitimate therapeutic technique for treating psychoneuroses and for relieving pain in surgery and childbirth.

Erickson Hypnotized With A Handshake

One of the 20th Century's greatest medical hypnotists was Milton Erickson. It is said that he could hypnotize a person just by holding his hand. As his reputation grew, there were colleagues of his that refused to shake his hand. Erickson differed on his views of hypnosis, not focusing on the hypnotist's power over the subject, but more of the hypnotist-subject relationship, attributing much to this "communication."

He believed every person was unique. Since Erickson was color-blind, tone deaf, twice paralyzed with polio, and dyslexic, he learned quickly to sympathize with others and to appreciate individual differences. He maintained everybody has the built-in inner resources needed to heal himself, that the hypnotic trance can break a person away from rigid self-defeating sets of mind and help restructure his inner resources in a positive, effective manner.

He also felt that hypnotic trance experiences are not separate from a person's normal behavioral pattern. They are like watching a movie, reading a novel, or daydreaming. Furthermore, he held that the unconscious mind can operate independently of the conscious mind and bring about major changes in thinking and feeling. As he said it, "Your conscious mind is very intelligent but your unconscious is a lot smarter."

Today, hypnosis, like a number of other "self-help" sciences, such as transcendental meditation, yogi, ESP, and Neurolingustic Programming (NLP) (except hypnotism enjoys the advantage of being blessed by the world medical community) is finding increased interest by people who simply want to experience it, and experience their inner selves.

Removing The Mystery Behind Hypnosis

"Look into my eyes. Deeper, deeper, deeper! You are now under my spell. You will do as I say."

Hypnosis has always been an enigma. A great deal has been written on the subject, yet much is contradictory. Like the blind men in the fable who endeavor to describe an elephant, a gray fog of ignorance still surrounds the basic workings of hypnosis.

"Look Into My Eyes..."

To many people, the image conjured up is one of a dark character, a bearded madman swinging a gold pocket watch in front of some innocent young soul, chanting in a forbidding, dark voice, *"Look into my eyes...,"* as the victim quickly falls into a stupored sleep, becoming mindlessly obedient, a zombie-like slave with no will to resist, blindly doing his bidding for him. Like cops and robbers shows on television, magnified and exaggerated, hypnotism is a distant reality from this distorted image.

I remember as a kid growing up in the 1950s, watching Sunday morning television. My sister and I would wait for the *Oral Roberts Show* to come on (one of TV's first ministers). When in the middle of his evangelical prayer service, he would invite some poor sick or crippled character on stage, and, as he looked up to the heavens, with his bare hand pressing hard against the believer's forehead, wildly shaking, almost in a jackhammer fashion, yell, *"HEAL BROTHER, HEAL!"* I'd be awestruck. As if it was scripted, the person would always appear instantly cured. The lame would throw away their canes, or get up from their wheelchairs, and walk. The blind would see, and the deaf would hear. Wow! Now I see how. *The power of the mind.* Hypnosis taps this power.

We All Encounter Hypnosis Daily

We all experience differing states of hypnosis everyday: when we become so totally engrossed in a television show or movie that we are oblivious to the outside world; when a child is hurt and the mother kisses the "boo-boo" to make it better; when the doctor prescribes a placebo to a patient and the person regains health; and the same goes for those that subscribe to the powers presumably vested in witch doctors and faith healers. Madison Avenue ad hucksters understand the power of suggestion. They try to influence our lives thousands of times a day: "Eat this, wear this, use this, buy me, no, buy ME, no, *BUY ME* -- and your life will be perfect!"

What Hypnosis Feels Like

The best example I can give of what hypnosis feels like to someone who has never experienced it firsthand, and I use this frequently in my preliminary talks with a subject, can be described this way: You know that feeling you get when, after a long, hard day, exhausted and while lying down on a sofa or bed, or maybe sitting back in a big, soft recliner chair, you begin to drift off, still conscious though in a fog, *a warm, floating feeling comes over your body?* That's hypnosis! Except, instead of it being momentary, of you wandering off to sleep, it stays with you. That's why many times subjects resist exiting their hypnotic state. *It feels too good.*

How Hypnosis Works

This book, you'll be happy to know, will avoid a long dissertation on the theoretical and scientific aspects of hypnosis. The world does not need another treatise on that subject. Some background, nevertheless, into how hypnosis works is in order. Let me preface this by saying that the following thoughts, since the jury is still out on all the scientific origins and causes of hypnosis, are formulating from my study of the subject, and represent my views on the subject.

Hypnosis is a way of getting directly into the subconscious mind. Hold that thought for a few moments.

Think of your brain as having three distinct levels, or states of consciousness: *active conscious, inactive conscious,* and *unconscious.*

The *unconscious* part of the brain is the *sleep* state. It *does not* play a role in hypnosis, at least not directly. Hypnosis only functions when the person is *awake.* Hypnotized people may look asleep, though they're not.

Hypnosis is the Opposite of Sleep

In fact, hypnosis is the *opposite* of sleep. In the sleep state, our attention is *defused.* We think/dream in wild, random patterns. Under hypnosis, our concentration is completely *focused.* Being able to focus all of our mind's ability so intently is what makes hypnotism work.

The *active conscious* part of the brain is where we do our *thinking*. When we're awake, our brain is functioning primarily in this level (although we can be in more than one level at a time, and usually are, to varying degrees).

All of our cognitive faculties rest here. When we decide to do something, or not to do something, it's because our active conscious mind tells us so.

The *inactive conscious* mind, or *subconscious*, is where all of our *learned* knowledge is stored (along with our egos, innate talents, and habits). Think of it, in a way, as the *library* we go to when we want to extract information that our active conscious mind uses in its decision-making process.

Habits are *learned* behaviors. If bits and pieces of *knowledge* learned and stored in the brain can be seen as *sentences* or paragraphs, *habits* are *chapters in a book*. Those habits that play a more consequential role in shaping our daily lives and personalities could be seen as entire books *or even tombs of books*.

Habits Hold The Key to Hypnosis

Habits can give insight into how hypnosis works. Habits rule our lives. From the moment we get up in the morning until the time we go to sleep at night, habits dictate most of what we do. They are the auto pilot mechanism in the brain. Let me give you a few examples. Did you ever find yourself blindly driving down a road, one you take frequently, say, going to school or work, when all of the sudden you realize you got there without making any conscious effort? How did it happen? Habit got you there. Say it's late at night and you decide to raid the refrigerator. As you enter the darkened kitchen, you instinctively reach for the light switch and flick it on. How did you know where it was in the dark? Habit. Or, how about this? You go to dial a phone number of a friend you talk to often, and without thinking of the number, your fingers press the buttons instinctively. Again, it was by habit.

How we form a habit is from the *cumulative effects of learned experiences*. In other words, if we do it enough, it becomes a habit. Smoking is a habit. Our speech pattern is a habit. How we walk is a habit. Habits, then, are *automatic*. If I was to say to you, how much is one plus one? You would immediately say, "Two." How did you know to say two? It's a learned experience. It came to you automatically, didn't it? You didn't have to give it any thought, and you *accepted it without judgment*. I said, "How much is one plus one?" You automatically replied, "Two."

Remember I said *hypnosis is a way of getting directly into the subconscious mind*? Hypnosis works because our subconscious mind accepts and processes information differently than our active conscious mind does. *The law of unconscious behavior demands that every idea, if it is subconsciously accepted, must automatically go into effect*. Whether the idea originates within the mind or is received from an outside source, is inconsequen-tial. Here is an example of external suggestion accepted and acted upon that you've probably experienced:

You're with a group of people. It's late in the evening. Someone yawns. You immediately yawn, too.

In essence, *hypnosis* is an *altered state of consciousness* in which *we manifest heightened suggestibility* and selective thought, *bypassing the critical evaluating facilities of the conscious mind*, the source of our judgmental, evaluative, and critical abilities.

Hypnosis is A Matter of Suggestibility

Hypnosis, then, is a matter of *suggestibility*, of having the subject accept what you say as fact, of allowing you into their subconscious mind. *At that point, what you say is as real and genuine as any learned knowledge they have.*

That, simply put, is how hypnosis works. In a hypnotized state, a subject told that a glass of water is a delicious cup of hot coffee can easily call up the experience of drinking coffee and believe it to be so. That person accepts the suggestion of water as coffee because, first, we've removed the barriers the active conscious (logical) mind would put up ("I can see that it's not coffee, doesn't smell like coffee, and it doesn't taste like coffee"), and second, our learned experiences about how coffee tastes can instantly be called upon to stimulate all the external senses we need to make the experience seem "real."

Mozart Knew How To Tap His Subconscious

Being able to tap into the subconscious is a potent tool. When asked how he was capable of writing such great music, Mozart said he only needed to close his eyes, relax his mind, and he was able to visualize the entire score of a new piece in finished form. The trick, he said, was to "wake up" from this state, and write the composition down. Otherwise he'd fall asleep, only to forget it all. Mozart was, in effect, practicing self-hypnosis.

Einstein Did, Too

Albert Einstein produced similar feats of brilliance. He said that the way he solved seemingly impossible problems was to relax in his recliner chair, close his eyes, and the answers would come to him automatically. We've all had this same experience. Have you ever had something troubling you, only to come up with the answer laying in bed, or to wake from a deep sleep in the middle of the night with a flash of genius? And if you didn't write it down, the answer was gone in the morning? If you've had that kind of experience, you've felt the power of hypnosis. It was Einstein who said that, *"Imagination is more important than knowledge."*

How Genius Works

Let's look a little more carefully at how Einstein was able to tap his genius. We know the brain is a vast memory bank. The human brain has approximately one hundred billion neurons, and each neuron has about a thousand synapses, or connections to other neurons. That translates to something on the order of *one hundred trillion* connections to the brain. The electrochemical impulses that pass through these synapses are the foundation of all of our feelings, concepts, ideas, and all mental experiences.

Conscious vs. Subconscious Mind

Our *conscious* mind, the left brain, processes information *logically* and *linearly*, literally in a straight line: 1, 2, 3, 4, 5, etc. It is *rational* and *organized*, and often referred to as the "analytic mind." The left brain also controls our voluntary (somatic) nervous system.

The *subconscious* mind, or right brain, on the other hand, sees *relationships in information* and processes them in *random, abstract patterns,* even when pieces to the answer are missing. The right brain is *creative, intuitive, irrational,* and *emotional.* The right brain controls our involuntary (autonomic) nervous system. Through *ideomotor* responses, or physical movements or behavior in response to an idea or thought in the mind, we can speed up or slow down our heart, and even alter the chemical balance in our body to fight off disease.

The two sides of our brain communicate with each other constantly, mixing logical, rational thoughts with the abstract and emotional, with emphasis in one hemisphere. Mathematicians are generally left brain people. Artists are generally right brain people. People of true genius know how to use both, with greater reliance on the right brain.

The new generation of computers, *parallel processors,* those used in artificial intelligence, work on this principal. Unlike linear computers that need all the parts to a puzzle, "neural networks," as they are sometime called, process whatever information is available to arrive at solutions. They effect *intuitive* solutions.

Einstein Put His Intuitive Abilities To Work

To arrive at his formula for energy, $E=mc^2$, Einstein used his *intuitive* abilities. Only *after* he arrived at his formula did he apply the complicated mathematical calculations needed to prove his theory. Einstein also intuited that time would move slower as speeds more closely approach the speed of light. It would take a few decades, not until superaccurate atomic clocks were developed, to prove him right. When told that his earlier postulations were right, he simply shrugged, as if to say, "So what else did you expect?"

Can We All Be Mozarts and Einsteins?

How powerful is *our* mind? Are we all capable of being Mozarts and Einsteins? Probably not. There is the little problem of innate intelligence. Still, we can all maximize the talent and intelligence we do possess. So how powerful is the average person's mind? Just how much more can we produce if we were able to use our minds to their full potential? Everyone has heard stories of a mother lifting a two-ton automobile off her trapped and injured child, or of people dying because they "lacked the will to live," or survived horrendous life-threatening situations because of "their will to live." Hypnosis is so exciting because it helps us reach this hidden wealth of mind talent like almost nothing else can.

A few years ago a scientific study was conducted where executives of large corporations were asked to use their intuitive abilities in guessing numbers picked by a computer. After waiting five years, the researchers went back to check on the subjects to see how they were doing with their businesses, and compared their financial results with their test scores.

Of the top 12 executives who doubled profits at their businesses, all had high test scores. Not too surprisingly, of the executives whose companies had not done as well, their test scores reflected this, with over half the subjects scoring below average. This study proves that in business, as in life, logic and reasoning go only so far. To really succeed, you need to use the power of your subconscious mind, too.

You Are The Bus Driver on The Road To The Subconscious Mind

Hypnosis, is a road to the subconscious mind. You are the bus driver taking the passenger on this pleasant journey. You choose the route, you hold the map in your hands, you steer the vehicle, they only need to look out the window and enjoy the scenery. Along the way, the bus may stop for the passenger to get off and experience certain things you point out to him or suggest he do. But, it's your bus, you can make it go where you want. The experience, however, is the manifestation of the subject's mind. That cup of coffee to one person may be a steamy hot cup of coffee from a paper cup, with big heaping spoonfuls of sugar. To someone else, it's an expresso in a demitasse cup with a lemon twist. That's one of the great things about hypnosis: each person experiences it in their own way.

Now the question becomes, *how do you get into the subconscious mind?* That's what you're about to learn.

Are You Left or Right Brain? An Easy Test.

By the way, there's a simple test you can take to determine if you're a left brain or right brain person. Interlock your fingers and thumbs, as if you are going to pray. After you do this, read the next paragraph. However, *don't read ahead until you interlock your fingers.*

With your fingers and thumbs now interlocked, look at the position of thumbs. If your left thumb is on top, you're a right brain person, and if your right thumb is on top, you're a left brain person. Why? Your right brain controls the left side of the body, and visa versa. The dominate hemisphere of your brain will always take charge.

Chapter

Testing

"Now feel me drawing you forward, feel that mysterious force pulling you towards me."

This chapter starts the process of learning the steps to hypnotism.

First you will learn to "test" the susceptibility of a person for induction into hypnosis, next you will learn various induction methods (Chapter 4), followed by deepening techniques to heighten the experience (Chapter 5), and then we go on to two chapters on routines you can use on hypnotized subjects. Chapter 8 shows you, step-by-step, how to conduct your own hypnotic stage show, and Chapter 9 is your introduction to self-hypnosis.

Testing Identifies Suggestibility

Testing is a way to prepare a subject for the more formal process of inducing hypnosis. Tests allow you to identify the *level of suggestibility* of a subject, the primary force in hypnosis. You may look at tests as *waking suggestions*, in many ways similar in nature to hypnotic suggestions. Tests give you a good indication as to how a subject may behave when being hypnotized, and assist you in determining which method to use in inducing the hypnotic condition. Tests can also help you to judge just how deep a state of hypnosis may be achieved.

Confidence is Key

Confidence in your ability to induce hypnosis is key. If the subject doesn't believe in your powers, he won't allow himself to be hypnotized. Therefore, *influencing* the subject into accepting your hypnotic ability, or *control* over that person, is very important. How they do on the actual tests is not all that you want to achieve, then. Being perceived as capable, the one in command of the situation, is just as material. Gain that person's confidence and you gain control of his mind and body.

As you become more familiar with hypnotizing subjects, and can judge their susceptibility and response, and as you develop a reputation for being a talented hypnotist, testing will not play as important a role in the hypnotic process. But, for now, let's learn some simple tests.

With all tests, you want to make certain that the subject feels he *wants* to perform well, that he doesn't fight your suggestions, or work hard to resist. One way to do that is to make testing a *positive challenge*. *"Let's see how much control your mind has over your body."* Or, *"Studies have shown that the smarter a person is, the more that person is able to focus his or her mind, and the better hypnotic subject they make."*

Let the person know that testing is not hypnosis. *"I'm going to try a few experiments to see how good you are at relaxing. I'm <u>not</u> going to try to hypnotize you."*

How To Start Out

When you start the testing, make certain that the subject realizes that his full attention and cooperation are needed, and that, assuming he follows your instructions carefully, he'll find the experience very stimulating. *"I assume you'd like to explore the full potential of your mind. With your permission, then, I'd like to try a few experiments. I only ask one thing of you: that you pay close attention to what I say and let things happen, or not happen, without interference on your part. Things may happen that you don't expect to happen or that I have not mentioned. If they do, let them happen."*

Try to keep the environment of the testing area simple. That means as few objects in the room as possible, open space to move around, and good lighting. If you try testing a person in a room cluttered with furniture and other things, it makes it that much more difficult to maintain the subject's full attention. He can be too easily distracted. You'll need some room to move around, so if necessary, remove some furniture. One thing you will need is a single, straight-back *armless* chair, plus one for yourself.

The "Hand Drop" Test

The *Hand Drop* test is a good place to start the testing process because it helps the subject to learn to relax. It also helps teach him to follow your commands. And, it's a simple test with easy-to-achieve results, so it should prove successful.

In hypnotism, *success breeds success*. If the subject sees the tangible results of following your commands, it builds his confidence in your ability, and with each experiment, step-by-step, that confidence and conditioning to respond to your commands grows stronger.

Start off by explaining, *"This is a simple relaxation test. Many people who think they are relaxed, really aren't."* Have the subject sit in the chair and extend his right hand out (forearm parallel with the ground) about a foot from his body, chest high, turning his wrist (at a 90 degree angle) upward with the index finger pointed up and the other fingers in a closed ball. The subject is then told to place the palm of his other hand squarely in the center of his right index finger.

"I want you to completely relax your left hand so that the entire weight of this hand and arm is supported solely by your right index finger. You need to be thoroughly relaxed, to let your left hand go limp. Concentrate, focus all your attention on relaxing your left hand. Let your right finger carry all the weight of your left hand." If it doesn't appear that the person is responding properly, reach over to his left elbow and lightly

move it up and down. If you feel any resistance, say, *"I can feel your hand is holding back. Relax completely, don't hold back."*

When you're satisfied that the subject is relaxed, say, *"I'm going to count to three, and when I say 'THREE,' I want you to IMMEDIATELY remove your right finger and your left hand will INSTANTLY fall down in your lap. Okay, one, relaxed completely, two, very lose, THREE!"*

In giving directions to a subject, always speak in a clear, calm, positive, monotone voice (except when emphasizing a word or phrase). Keep your voice pleasant, but yet firm. Let there be no question of your authority and the fact that you expect the subject to respond to your commands.

If the subject's hand falls in his lap, say, *"Excellent,"* and move on to the next exercise. If he fails this test, explain that, *"Many times when we believe we are relaxed, we're not. You just proved that. The ability to achieve success is in direct proportion to your ability to relax. The mind is very powerful. When an idea is held strongly enough, it tends to realize itself in unconscious movements. So relax, don't think too much about it, and you'll do great!"*

At this point, try the test over again, making certain the person has the full weight of his left hand on the right finger. If the test fails twice, use *your* right finger for the test, and don't remove it until you're certain you're fully holding the weight of his hand.

The "Pendulum Swing" Test

This is another good test to start out with. Have the subject sit in the chair. You'll need a pendulum, which you can make with a piece of string, about two feet long. On one end tie a weight (like a fisherman's weight), a pocket watch, metal washer, or any similar object. Hand the pendulum to the subject, asking him to hold it at the top of the string between his thumb and index finger. Have the person then rest the elbow of the hand holding the pendulum on his leg, just above the knee, suspending the pendulum between his two feet, which should be spread apart. Leaning forward, the person should have the pendulum dangling above the ground, with enough space around it to freely move.

Holding the object attached to the string so that it cannot move, you say, *"In a few seconds, I'm going to release my hand, when I do, I want you to focus all of your attention on the (object)...At all times I want you to keep your eyes on the (object). I'm letting go of the (object)...now. Okay, I want you to see the (object) swaying back and forth, rocking back and forth, moving forward and backward, and as you do, you'll see it follow your mind's thoughts. Don't force it to happen. But if it does, just let it happen. "Back...and forth...forward and backward...to...and fro..."*

If you see movement in the pendulum, continue the directions, *"Now the (object) is swinging farther back and forth, it's moving farther and farther out..."*

If the motion of the pendulum is not as you directed, say, *"Or it can move in a (circle or left to right)..."*

If you're getting good results, try to get the movement to change. *"Now I want you to imagine the (object) swinging around in a circle, picture it moving around and around, it's changing from its back and forth motion, its starting to circle around...the circle is getting bigger, its moving faster..."*

Once you get the desired affects, grab a hold of the object and say, *"That was perfect. Let's try something else."*

The "Hands Up" Test

Have the subject stand facing you. Say, *"Please stand with your feet shoulder-width apart. At no time during this experiment will I (or anyone else) touch you in any way, unless I tell you first. Before we start, and don't do anything yet, just watch what I do."*

You should be standing opposite the subject with your feet in the same position you want the subject to be in (normal stance). Slowing lift both of your hands straight up to their sides, lifting both hands at the same time. When your hands are at shoulder level, briefly pause for a few seconds, stop, look at the subject and say, *"Now I want you to close your eyes."* When the person's eyes are closed, *"I want you to picture the way my hands were rising in the air. Now concentrate on YOUR hands. Picture your hands like wings on a bird. The more you concentrate on your hands, the more you may feel like they are getting LIGHTER, and if you concentrate hard enough you'll feel them actually LIFTING up, like I just showed you. Don't force anything to happen, but if it does, just allow it to happen. Again, picture your hands getting very light, forget about everything else, only listen to my voice and focus all your attention on your hands. As you feel your hands getting lighter, and one hand may feel lighter than the other, or they may both feel light together, just allow them to drift up. And as your hands rise, you will notice that as they rise, the more they do rise the lighter they'll get."*

If the subjects hands are rising, continue to give them additional suggestions. *"Your hands are feeling very light, lighter, lighter, lighter...drifting higher, higher, higher!* Once the person's hands have moved up in the air, stop the test. *"Okay, I want you to stop lifting your hands now. But leave them in the position they're in. Now open your eyes and observe what's happened to your hands."* By seeing their hands in the air, you reinforce this power you have. Ask the subject to now relax their hands, allowing them to drop back down by his side.

If you feel that the subject has sufficiently responded to your commands and that they were easily controlled into following your suggestions, you may wish to move directly to inducing hypnosis (next chapter).

If the subjects hands have not risen, try saying, *"Imagine that I'm attaching a giant helium balloon on a string to each one of your wrists. I'm going to be touching your wrists now one at a time."* You will approach the subject, *"I'm attaching one balloon to your left wrist now."* As you say this reach over with your thumb and index finger and lighter swipe your fingers around the person's wrist, gently removing your hands as you complete the action. Now do the other hand. *"I want you to picture the balloons, and imagine that they are filled with helium, that the balloons are straining to rise into the air, and as they do, you feel the strings I tied to your wrists pulling, tugging on your hands, making your arms very light. A giant helium balloon attached to each of your wrists. Picture your hands getting lighter, picture the strings pulling on your wrists, allowing your hands to rise up, up, up! Concentrate, focus all your attention on your hands, picture them getting lighter and lighter!"*

If this doesn't produce any results, say, *"I've just attached another helium balloon to each wrist, and this one is BIGGER that the other one. Your hand is going to start to feel very light now, your hand is going to want to rise up in the air. And as it does, you're just going to let it. You're not going to force it to happen. It will happen on its own. Feel your hand getting lighter, feel the string pulling your hand up..."*

If the subject begins to respond in any way, keep telling the person you're adding more and more balloons. Do this until you get the desired results.

If no response is shown after a few minutes, stop the test. Don't let the subject know you didn't get the results you wanted, or that he was less than perfect in his test. Dismiss it all by saying you're going on to the next test. *"Okay, you can stop now and open your eyes. That was very good. Now let's try something else."*

This exercise points out the subtle differences in how you word a command. If you say, for instance, *"You are raising your hand,"* versus, *"Your hand is rising,"* the latter will achieve much better results. It makes the suggestion *non-voluntary.* The subject is thinking, "I'm not doing it, it's my *hand* that is making it happen." It may seem like a minor point, but it has great significance in eliciting proper responses.

If the subject fails to raise his hands in this test, and you want to "help" the process along, here's something you can do.

Ask the person to stand in a narrow doorway, hands at his side. Keeping his arms straight, have him press the backs of his hands against the door frame with all his strength, as though he is trying to push the frame out. Have him exert this force for ten to fifteen seconds and count out loud, as you say, *"Keep pressing your hands...pressing out...harder... harder...keep pressing..."*

As he reaches the last number, ask him to step forward, away from the door, and *just as he does,* raise your arms up to shoulder height as you say, *"Watch as your hands get s-o light they rise up...they're as light as a feather, aren't they?* You'll notice his arms will rise up like an elevator, caused by a natural muscle response. To the subject though, it will be very convincing.

The "Hand Magic" Test

The *Hand Magic* Test is another good test to perform. It involves having the subject hold his hand out in front about twelve inches from his face, palm facing in, and the fingers held together pointed upward.

"I'd like you to pick a spot in the middle of your hand (feel free to actually touch the spot you want that person to stare at) *and focus all your attention there. As you concentrate, and again, forget about anything or anyone else in the room, only listen to*

the sound of my voice...you may notice a couple of things. First, you may notice that your fingers will want to separate and open up. And secondly, you may notice that your hand will feel like it wants to move in towards your face. If either or both of these things begin to happen, let them. Don't force it to happen. But if it does, just allow it to happen. Right now, as you focus all your attention on that one spot, you may find it difficult to do. Shapes and colors may begin to emanate out from that spot. Your eyes may begin to hurt. Keep focused. Only think of that one spot. As you do, imagine a force, an invisible force lightly pushing on the back of your hand, drawing it in towards your face. If it feels like it wants to move in towards your face, let it. Don't force it to happen. But if it does, just allow it to happen. You may also find it hard to keep your fingers together. If they feel like they want to separate, let them. Don't force it to happen. But if it does, just allow it to happen."

Watch for signs of either the fingers separating or the hand being drawn in. If the subject is experiencing either or both actions, take advantage of it. Say, for instance, you see the subject's hand being drawn in. You might offer, *"Concentrate on your hand being drawn in towards your face. You can feel the invisible force working, and as your hand moves in towards your face, the more it moves, the easier and faster it will happen."* Or, assuming you see a finger or the thumb move, *"You may feel your thumb wants to move away from your fingers. Just let it."* By the way, if the subject seems to be reacting differently than your commands, say his thumb begins twitching, then you want to say, *"I see your thumb is moving. I wonder what it will do next?"*

If the subject is resisting or shows no signs of movement, encourage him to concentrate more. *"Relax, don't try to force any movement, but I'd like you to think about your fingers, think about your fingers wanting to separate, of moving apart, and as you do, you will find it harder and harder to keep them together."*

This experiment, like the *Hands Up* test should take only a few minutes. If you're getting good results early on, shorten up the test and move on to the next, or if the results you're getting are very positive, go directly to the induction of hypnosis (next chapter). If the results are not as expected, try relaxing the subject, assuring him that if he concentrates enough, and trusts you, the results will be there.

Again, never tell a subject he has failed a test or is not producing good results. If you have to, blame the conditions, the room, the lightening, etc. If he feels it's his fault, his concentration will be misplaced. The best state of mind for a subject is total relaxation and trust.

The 'Falling Forwards - Falling Backwards" Test

This is actually a two-part test. Part one is the falling backwards experiment.

Have the subject stand up erect, with his back to you, feet together, hands by his side. With both your hands, one at the subject's forehead and the other at the nap of his neck, gently lean the person's head back. *"I'd like you to remain as relaxed as possible, and tilt your head back (this has the effect of slightly offsetting the person's natural equilibrium) and hold it in this position, if you will."* While you're doing this make certain the subject is relaxed. Do this by holding the person's shoulders and slowly pulling him back. If he comes back easily, he is relaxed. If he's not, remind him to relax.

"Now close your eyes. At any time during this experiment, you have the sensation of falling backwards, don't worry, I'm standing right behind you, and I'll hold you up. In a few seconds I'm going to place both of my hands on your forehead. As I slowly remove them, you will likely feel a sensation of falling backwards. If you do feel like falling back, let it happen. Don't force it to happen. But if it does, just allow it to happen. I'll catch you."

I should point out that many words and expressions used in these tests are repeated. That's all part of *conditioning*, getting subjects used to responding to certain commands. Most of the commands are passive. It's not the old, *"You are falling back!"* If you said that, and the person has no urge to fall back, then you lose credibility. The subject sees you failing. By saying something like, *"When you feel like falling backward..."* you don't make the test a clear win-or-lose.

"Okay, I'm going to put my hands on your forehead now." As you do, place them fingertip-to-fingertip across the person's temple, with the hands meeting in the middle. *"As I remove my hands, you may feel the sensation of falling backwards. If you do, just allow yourself to fall back, and I'll catch you."*

Very slowly and with the gentlest of touch, bring both your hands back, drawing them back across the temple, just above the ears, and then downward towards the back of the neck, and finally drawing them back, lifting them off ever so softly and slowly. Stand ready, with your hands out in front of you about one foot from the subject's back ready to catch him.

"Feel yourself wanting to fall backwards, feel the mysterious force driving your body back, ever so gently, you feel yourself falling backwards. I'm here, I'll catch you. Anytime you do feel like falling back, let it happen. Don't force it to happen. But if it does, just allow it to happen."

If you see the subject start to sway backwards, play it up. *"You feel it. You feel you're wanting to fall back. Go ahead, allow yourself to fall back into my arms!"* If it appears that the person is resisting, urge him to relax. *"Don't fight your inner feelings. Let go! If you want to fall back, do it!"*

Either way, allow about a half-minute at most for the subject to respond to your commands. If you get a good response, re-enforce it by repeating the test, except, this time, have the subject face you.

In the falling forwards experiment, have the subject stand directly in front of you, again, feet together. You should be standing with your feet about shoulder-width apart and one foot just in back of the other. *"This time I'm going to ask you to concentrate and imagine the feeling of falling forward, towards me. If you do, I'll catch you, so don't worry."*

Stare the subject directly in the face, but instead of looking at the person eyeball-to-eyeball, center your attention at the bridge of the person's nose, in a spot just below and between the subject's eyebrows. Placing both your hands behind and above the person's ears, fingertips lightly touching the subjects head, repeat, *"I'd like you to look into my eyes. I want you to think about the sensation of falling forward. If, at any time you do feel like falling forward, let it happen. Don't force it to happen. But if it does, just allow it to happen. I'll catch you."*

Still staring intently at the subject (and make certain the subject is constantly staring at you, and if not, direct him to do so) slowly allow your fingers to be drawn forward towards you, stopping for a second on the person's temple, and then very lightly lifting them off his head. As you draw your hands back, do so in a slightly downward motion, fingers spread, palms facing the subject, until they stop to each side of your face, about chin level, and a foot away. Your hands should be just in the visual field of the subject. In as subtle a way as possible, with your actions not being too obvious, lean your body back very, very *slowly*, imperceptibly in fact, back about six to twelve inches. All the movement should be from the waist up.

"Now feel me drawing you forward, feel that mysterious force pulling you towards me. If you do feel like falling forward, let it happen. Don't force it to happen. But if it does, just allow it to happen. I'll catch you. Feel yourself being drawn forward..."

Continue the suggestions for no more than a half-minute. If the subject falls forward, tell him, *"Excellent, you're doing great."* If he doesn't fall, and say he hasn't done well on any of the previous tests, you will need to discuss the "block" this person has. Maybe he's nervous, or doesn't fully understand what kind of response to give. Generally, though, you can be fairly certain that subjects who respond well in testing will respond equally well in the hypnosis process. The reverse is usually true, too. If a subject is resisting you all the way, don't try to hypnotize that person. Instead, say, *"I don't think the conditions are right today for us to proceed. I get a strong feeling you are inwardly fighting me. Let's try this another time."*

The "Hands Together" Test

Here's a final test to use only with *very responsive* subjects. Request the subject stand in front of you, and extend his arms out, clasping his hands together interlocking the fingers. *"I want you to lock your fingers together as tightly as you possibly can. Now extend your hands out completely. Feel your elbows locking. Tight. Tighter. VERY TIGHT."* Have the subject stare into your eyes as you gaze intently into his (as described above in the Falling Forward experiment).

"I want you to focus all your attention inward. I want you to THINK about your fingers locking into one another. The more you concentrate, the more you'll find your hands have LOCKED in this position. I want you to say to yourself, 'My hands are LOCKED in place, I can't move my fingers. I can't get my hands apart.' Feel the power of your hands LOCKING TOGETHER! Imagine, if you will a giant magnet has drawn your hands together, and they're unable to separate" As you say this, take your hands and firmly, yet not with physical force, press his hands together.

"I'm going to count to ten, and as I do, you will feel your hands drawing even tighter together. By the time I reach the count of ten, you will find it IMPOSSIBLE to unlock your fingers and separate your hands...until I tell you that you can. "Ready?...One...fingers locking together...two...hands being drawn

tighter...three...four...tighter, tighter still...five...very tight...six...hands feel STUCK together...seven...fingers locked tight...EIGHT...you can't move your hands apart...NINE...TEN...HANDS LOCKED, FINGERS LOCKED...you can't separate your hands! I'm going to remove my hands now, and as I do, I want you to try to slowly separate your hands." Give the person only a few seconds to try and separate his hands.

If the person's hands stay locked together, say, *"Stop trying to separate your hands. I'm going to count to three and when I clap my hands, you'll INSTANTLY be able to separate your hands. One, two, THREE (clap your hands), hands SEPARATE!"*

If the person's hands do separate, ask him what the experience felt like. A lot of times, while the outward signs did not produce desired affects, the subject may have experienced inner feelings. It's always good to ask the person, *"So what were you experiencing?"* or *"When I told you to do ____, what did it feel like?"*

While we're on this subject, it is very important that you never allow the subject to feel he has "beaten" the test. If you see he is about to separate his hands when you have just told him he won't be able to, immediately say, *"Now you can separate your hands."* In a positive tone, like it was expected, add, *"You had a little bit of trouble separating your hands, didn't you?"* Remember, no matter what happens, it should appear that the response was normal and expected.

Some Concluding Thoughts

Hypnosis may be a science, yet many times it's the art in what you do that makes the difference. Don't look at the language above as a *script* to be memorized, or the techniques offered as *formulas* with consistent results. Many times you'll need to ad lib, to go "off-the-script." That's where practice and experience pays off. It's good to practice your testing techniques thoroughly, using a willing subject or two, before you attempt to move further into hypnosis.

One other thought. Don't get so caught up in what you're doing that you forget about the subject. You need to constantly monitor the person and factor his response, or lack of response, into your work. *The situation should always dictate the course of action, not the other way around.*

When you feel confident with this section, you can move on to the most fascinating part of hypnosis, inducing the hypnotic state.

The Five Rules of Testing

1. ALWAYS CANCEL ANY SUGGESTION GIVEN BEFORE GIVING ANOTHER. If you told the person he would not be able to bend his arm, remove the suggestion first, before going on to another test: *"You can now bend your arm."*

2. BE CONFIDENT. For a suggestion to be accepted and locked in the subconscious mind it must bypass the critical facilities of the conscious mind. To be that convincing requires absolute confidence and self-assurance.

3. __HYPNOSIS IS AS MUCH ART AS SCIENCE__. Don't look at the language in this book as a script. Be prepared to ad lib.

4. __MAKE TESTING A POSITIVE CHALLENGE__. The objective here is to make the subject feel he wants to perform well, not to fight your suggestions or work hard to resist.

5. __PRACTICE MAKES PERFECT__. Don't expect to be a professional the first time out. Practice, experiment, work at being a successful hypnotist like you would expect to have to work to perfect any skill.

Chapter

Inducing A Trance

"With every breath you take, with every beat of your heart...you will find yourself going deeper and deeper to sleep...drifting deeper and deeper, d-e-e-p-e-r and d-e-e-p-e-r..."

Up to this point, everything you've been doing with the subject has been in the *waking* state. Now we move on, delving into his subconscious mind, by inducing the hypnotic condition, or hypnotic trance. This is where *the fun begins!*

I will show you four different induction techniques that all work very effectively. While there are literally hundreds of induction methods, the ones shown here incorporate many of the basic principles of all inductions.

The "Eye Fixation" Method

Let's start with my favorite, and one that's a proven standard, the *Eye Fixation* method.

By now, the subject should be well conditioned to react as you desire to commands given. Make certain you have advised the person that: he has nothing to fear; he will not fall asleep, and at all times will be fully awake and conscious of everything happening to him; you will do nothing to harm him, and, in fact, being hypnotized is a wonderful-feeling experience, so he should sit back, relax, and enjoy it; and finally, to gain the maximum out of this encounter, he must concentrate intently on everything you say, and be open to take all your suggestions freely and willingly.

"In a minute or two we're going to begin the next phase of our experiments. Before we start, though, I would like to describe to you what's about to take place. First of all, you will be conscious throughout the entire session, and you will hear everything I say to you. You will feel something different about yourself, however, a sort of heightened awareness of your mind and body. That's good, because the most important thing for you to remember, is that if you open your mind to all I have to say, accept the ideas without question, let whatever happens happen, you'll do great! In fact, the best way to help me is to just listen to what I say and let whatever you feel is going to happen or is happening to happen, without interference. It may not be what you expect. That's all right. Don't force it to happen. But if it does, just allow it to happen."

Two things you'll notice about what I just said: I never used the word "hypnotize," and I spoke only in positive tones. It's perfectly okay to use the word "hypnotize," but be careful that you not say it in such a way that it puts up a challenge. *"I'm about to hypnotize you,"* immediately challenges that person to be hypnotized. You'll probably get one of two reactions: either, "I'm too strong to be hypnotized, so just let'em try. I'll resist!" Or, "Okay, I'm ready to be hypnotized. When is it going to happen? It's not happening yet...I'm waiting!" You'll also note the positive tone in my words, *"...you will feel..."* and the spirit of cooperation involved, *"...the best way to help me..."*

If the subject is not seated, have him take a (armless) seat in the chair. He should be sitting upright, his feet on the ground, with his hands placed lightly on each leg.

"I want you to sit comfortably in this chair, feet firmly planted on the ground, with your hands, palm down, resting lightly each hand on each one of your legs."

The room you've chosen for this should be free of distractions, particularly within the field of vision of the subject. This includes objects on the wall directly in front of him. The room should have a normal amount of light. Avoid having the primary illumination coming from an overhead light that is in front of the subject. That can be very distracting. Try to position the subject's chair so that he is about ten or so feet from the wall he is facing.

At a level high enough that the person must turn his eyes up to look, you should have already placed a small, bright object for him to focus on: a thumb tack (my favorite), button, or similar object held on the wall with double-faced tape. You may want to fashion something, a small circle, out of paper. Make sure the color of this object contrasts the wall. A bright white thumb tack on a white wall is obviously no good.

As you're talking to the subject, you should be positioning yourself off to the side, just out of the way of his field of vision, so as not to distract him. Try remaining in a stationary position to minimize extraneous noise. Avoid walking around. You may wish to even sit in a chair.

"Do you see that small object (let's assume from now on it's a button) *I've placed on the wall over there? I want you to keep your eyes on it, to look at it all the while I'm talking. Pay close attention only to the button, and listen carefully to my words. Do not permit any other thoughts to enter your mind. Forget the rest of the world. Give up the outside world. Think only of what I say, and focus only on that button. If, at any time, your eyes should wander off the button, don't worry. Just bring your eyes back to it. You may see shapes or colors emanating out from the button, the button may get bigger or smaller, it may start moving, a halo may appear around it, or it may get very blurry, or vanish. Whatever happens, let it happen.*

"Oh, let me remind you now that at anytime your eyes get so tried they want to close, go right ahead. You don't need me to tell you. You can close them anytime you want.

"Right now, while you watch the button, I want you to begin to notice your body relaxing. As you concentrate, the more you do, you will begin to feel your whole body relax...every muscle will free itself of any stress or tension...your head is beginning to relax, your neck and shoulders...down your arms...throughout your back...into your feet.

As you focus your attention more and more, you'll notice your legs getting very heavy, your whole body will begin to sink into the chair...your feet will be rooted to the floor."

It is impossible to give you a precise word-for-word script to follow, since all subjects react differently. I've had people who were under hypnosis and I wasn't even finished telling them it was okay to close their eyes when they wanted to! And some people take fifteen minutes or more. That's why it's always important to look for feedback from the subject. Remember what I told you before: You need to constantly monitor the person and factor his response, or lack of response into your work. *The situation should always dictate the course of action, not the other way around.*

Feel free to use the person's name, too. *"Bill, I want you to fix your eyes on the button...as you do, you will feel that your whole body is getting relaxed...your muscles are getting relaxed...you can feel a heaviness coming over your whole body...your feet and legs are getting very heavy...you feel your body sinking deeper into the chair...it feels very good...now I want you to concentrate on your hands...they are feeling very heavy, too...at any time you feel that they are getting so heavy that they want to move off your legs and fall down by your side, I want you to let them. Don't force it to happen, but if one or both of your hands feel like falling down by your side, you can let it happen...think about your fingers...they are getting very heavy...they feel very relaxed...you may feel that they may want to slide off your legs and help your arms fall down by your sides...if they do, you should let them...don't force it to happen, but if it does, just let it happen.*

"Think of sleep...think about how it feels to be asleep...think about how tired your eyes are becoming...your eyes may burn...feel tired...feel heavy..."

When you're working with commands as specific as asking that the person's hands fall off to the side, you need to pay very close attention to any signs, any signals of reaction to your words. If, for instance, you see the subject's left hand start to twitch, or a finger or thumb starts to move, adapt your induction speech to fit. Let's assume the subject's left thumb is moving slightly. *"As this heaviness falls over your body, you may feel one of your hands wants to move off your lap more than the other. Or, maybe you feel a thumb or finger wanting to lift off. Concentrate, focus on this hand...feel it wanting to lift off...feel your thumb wanting to lift and slide your hand off to the side..."*

Don't be concerned about whether the person's hand or hands do fall off to the side. The object is to move that person into his subconscious mind, and the hands falling down are only a manifestation of that action taking place, it's a signal that you've reached a certain level in the induction process. If you don't get the desired effects within a minute or two, move on to other areas.

"You may be noticing that the more you relax, the more you focus on the button, how heavy and tired your eyes are getting. Remember, anytime your eyes get so tried you want to close them, allow them to close. You don't need me to tell you. Your eyes can close anytime they want...focusing intently now on the button...relax every muscle in your body...relax your legs...relax your feet...relax your arms...relax your hands...relax your fingers...relax your eyes...your eyes are getting heavy....your eyes are feeling very tired....your eyes are starting to blink more (time this to actual blinking)...*each time your eyes blink you will find it gets harder to open them...with each effort, it will get harder and harder to keep your eyes open...when they get so heavy that you can't keep them open, I want you to allow them to close...and when they do close, they will want to*

remain closed...and you will let them...your eyes are burning now...they're getting very blurry...they are so-o heavy you can hardly keep them open...with every breath you take, with every beat of your heart, you will find yourself drifting off...your body getting very relaxed...very heavy...it feels very good..."

Again, the eyes closing, like the arms falling by the side, are signs of the person slipping into the subconscious state. If he is not responding to your commands, you need to improvise. Always keep your voice level even, and speak in a calm, cool, monotone. Never seem surprised. Act as though whatever is happening is what you expect to happen. Throughout this induction process, work on three areas of the body: the eyes closing, the hands falling by the side, and the feet feeling firmly planted on the ground. The latter, however, will not give you the same physical manifestations.

I can't stress enough, you will need to modify your speech according to what the subject does or doesn't do. For instance, using the eye example, you don't want to send mixed or confusing signals. If you keep talking about the subject starring at the button, and his eyes have already closed, it will interfere with the flow, and probably slowdown or even ruin the induction.

Stay alert. Be empathetic. Try to feel what the subject is feeling. You'll find it will greatly improve your ability to keep the tempo of the induction speech in tune, so to speak, with how the subject is thinking and reacting. Occasionally, I find myself briefly closing *MY EYES* trying to picture not only what the subject is feeling outwardly, but what all his inner senses may be feeling: what he sees, what he hears, what his mind and body are experiencing.

You don't want to force a person to close his eyes until he is ready. The one exception is where a person has given a number of outside signs of being hypnotized, but his eyes remain open. It's possible in certain subjects that they can be fully hypnotized but their eyes remain open. In this case you can say, *"Your eyes are very tired...it's okay to close them now...that's right, allow your eyes to close...and allow them to stay closed...very good!"*

Here are some outward signs or signals to look for that indicate that the subject is entering the trance state: A noticeably change in the breathing pattern -- heavier and slower; a general lethargy or slowness in movement; the body becoming limp; and a visible sweatiness.

Many people under hypnosis actually can feel their body's system changing as they gain a heightened awareness of their inner self. Many times, when you see the outward signs, you might say, *"You might notice your breathing feels like it's slowing down...this is normal...its your body in a more relaxed state..."*

When the subject's eyes have not closed after a reasonable time, you might say, *"Keep staring at the button, allow your eyes to focus on that one spot...keep looking at the button even though your eyes are getting more and more tired..."* This acknowledges that his eyes are open, but it's okay. At all times, watch for any other signs of anxiety or discomfort that may be interfering with the induction. If there are noises coming from outside the room, remind the subject, *"Forget the outside world, focus ONLY on the button and listen ONLY to my words..."*

If after closing his eyes, a subject should open them, tell him, *"You just proved that you're not FULLY relaxed, I want you to close your eyes, to close them tightly* (make sure the subject is complying) *and to think of nothing but sleep, deep, deep, s-l-e-e-p!..."*

With some people, upon entering the early stages of hypnosis, upon closing their eyes, find their head getting very tired. Let's assume the subject has just closed his eyes. As it's happening, *"Your eyes are closing now, they are closing very tight...it feels very good to close your eyes...notice now, if you will, that your head and neck will begin to relax even more, that with every breath you take, you will feel the muscles in your head, neck, and shoulder relax...they're getting very relaxed...any time you want to, you may allow your head to move forward and rest in your chest, or off to the side...if you feel that your head wants to rest down in front of you or lean off to the side, let it. Don't force it to happen, but if it does, just allow it to happen...Your head is getting very heavy...it wants to nod forward...to move down...your neck muscles are very relaxed...it's getting harder and harder to keep your head up...."*

Assuming the person's head does fall down in his chest or off to the side, channel that back to encourage other actions. Success breeds success. If the subject is responding to something you're saying, use it as a building block to achieve other things. *"Very good...now that you're more relaxed, I want you to concentrate on your hands. With every breath you take, with every beat of your heart, you will find yourself becoming more and more relaxed, falling deeper and deeper into the state of relaxation you're feeling now...feel your hands getting very heavy...very heavy...heavier. Very shortly your hands, either both of them or one of them will begin to lift up or slide off to the side. Maybe your thumb will be first, or you may feel something in one of your fingers. I wonder what will happen first?*

"As you concentrate more and more, you will find your hands getting extremely heavy, it will be hard for them to stay resting on your legs...and when they do fall off to your side, your hands will feel very good...and you will find yourself going into an even deeper and deeper state of relaxation, much deeper and more enjoyable than what you're feeling now...feel your hands falling off to the side...getting heavy...heavy...very heavy...".

Once the person's arms fall off to the side, as with the head movement, use that to move on to the legs. *"Your hands are feeling very good...your body is becoming more and more relaxed...with every breath you take, with every beat of your heart, you can feel yourself sinking deeper and deeper into the state of relaxation you're in...you can feel your legs getting very heavy now...they're sinking into the floor...your knees feel like someone placed a bag of cement across them...they're so heavy you don't want to move them...you could move them if you tried hard enough...but you don't want to...they feel so good. It's like your feet (shoes) are glued to the floor...you won't be able to move them or lift them up..."*

At this stage, the subject should be in a hypnotized state. He may be in a light trance or under deeply. They're are some tests and deepening techniques you can use now to determine the level of trance the person is in and to deepen it.

One test is to have the subject try to lift up his legs. Here's how you can do that: *"In a few minutes we're going to try something. I'm going to ask you to do something, BUT DON'T DO ANYTHING YET, UNTIL I ASK YOU TO....In a few minutes, as I said, I'm going to ask you to try to lift up your legs. You're going to find it very hard to do. In fact, it will be s-OO hard to lift your legs that you won't want to...I want you to concentrate on your legs. Feel them getting heavier...and heavier...and heavier...AND HEAVIER...with every breath you take, with every beat of your heart, your body will fall deeper and deeper into the state of relaxation it's in...legs getting heavy...feet very heavy...Okay, now when I ask you, I want you to try to lift your left leg up... When I ask you to try and lift it up, start by trying to lift from your knee, try to lift your leg off the ground...as you do, though, you'll find it's so hard to lift your leg, you won't want to, that your leg will remain rooted to the floor, like its glued to the floor...okay, when I say three, try to slowly, very SLOWLY lift your left leg...one...two...three...you're trying to lift your knee, your foot is too heavy..."* Don't let the person try to lift his foot for more than four or five seconds.

"All right STOP! Don't try to lift your leg anymore. That was very good. Relax, let your body drift off into a state of relaxation deeper than it's in now...drifting deeper and deeper... d-e-e-p-e-r and d-e-e-p-e-r...more and more relaxed. Good, now let's try the other leg. Like before, DON'T TRY TO LIFT YOUR RIGHT LEG UNTIL I ASK YOU TO. In a few moments, I'm going to ask you to try to lift up your right leg. When I ask you to try and lift it up, again start by trying to lift from your knee, try to lift your leg off the ground...as you do, though, you'll find it's so hard to lift your leg you won't want to, that your right foot is even heavier than your left foot...that the more you try, the more your leg will remain rooted to the floor, like it's glued to the floor...and even more amazing, that after you try to lift your leg, that when I ask you to stop trying, and to relax, you will find yourself falling deeper and deeper into the state of relaxation than you're in now...deeper and deeper...okay, when I say three, try to slowly, very SLOWLY lift your right foot...one...two... three...you're trying to lift your knee, your foot is too heavy..."

Again, don't let the person try to lift his foot for more than a few seconds. *"All right STOP!. Don't try to lift your leg anymore...drifting deeper and deeper to sleep...DEEPER and DEEPER into this state of relaxation you're in...deeper and deeper...just allow yourself to drift off...with very breath you take, with every beat of your heart, you will find yourself sinking deeper and deeper into this wonderful, wonderful sleep...sleep...s-l-e-e-p."*

Should the subject's leg start to lift at anytime, you should immediately tell them, *"Okay, relax your leg. Stop trying to lift it. You can feel how heavy it is to lift it up...don't try anymore."*

Two expressions used in this speech, *state of relaxation* and *sleep,* are euphemisms for hypnosis, but, again, we want to avoid saying *"You are hypnotized."*

You should be able to freely speak with the subject now. For instance, you might want to ask them about lifting their leg. *"Your leg was very heavy, wasn't it?"* or, *"What did it feel like when you tried to lift your leg?"* Most will respond with a slowness in their speech and a heaviness in the tone. This is normal for this condition.

Something else to keep in mind is the tone and manner of your voice. Any inflections, changes in audible level, pauses...adding a question mark...or other features of speech play a big role in how the meaning of words and sentences are interpreted. For example, you could say, *"Your arm is stiff and rigid, you cannot bend it. Try to bend it,"* or, you could say the same thing like this, *"Your arm is STIFF and RIGID. You cannot bend it. TRY to bend it!"*

There are several other deepening techniques you can apply here, but let's save those for the next chapter. Right now, let's look at another induction technique, the *Arm Levitation* method.

The "Arm Levitation" Method

From a practical standpoint, you will probably find one induction technique that works best for you, and use it almost exclusively. That's fine. You don't need to employ any more induction methods if you're having success with one. The *Eye Fixation* method is a good example. It has been around since Braid developed it some 150 years ago (Hollywood embellished upon it 100 years later, by inventing the swinging pocket watch gimmick for the movies).

Here's another standard, the *Arm Levitation*.

You might want to use this procedure with subjects who have responded well to the *Hands Up* and *Hand Magic* test. In fact, you will notice a great deal of similarity between the *Arm Levitation* method of induction and the *Hand Magic* test.

With the person seated, hands on his lap (or you could have the dominant hand resting on a table or arm of a chair), say, *"I want you to completely relax, to allow your mind to focus only on what I'm about to say...give up the outside world...only listen to my voice...accept the ideas I offer without question, let whatever happens happen. Don't force it to happen. But if it does, just allow it to happen...Now I want you to concentrate all of your attention on your (right) hand. If, at any time your eyes should wander off your hand, don't worry. Just bring your eyes back to it...In a few moments you may begin to notice things about your hand that were not evident before...these are things that have always happened, but possibly you've never noticed them so closely before...you may feel a pressure on your hand against your leg (table, chair, etc.)...you may be aware of the texture of the fabric (wood, metal, etc.)...or, perhaps your hand will begin to feel cold...or warmth...yes, a warmth through your hand...a nice glowing feeling...feel the warmth of your hand...and as your hand becomes more aware of this warm feeling, another tingling sensation is starting to appear...can your hand feel it?...You may even feel your fingers begin to twitch...and as this feeling grows, you will become aware of a tension developing in your arm....it will grow too....it will feel as though something is about to happen with your hand..."*

Like before, you need to watch for any overt signs of the subject responding, and where necessary, to modify your induction speech accordingly. Let's assume for the moment that the person is responding well, taking your suggestions without resistance, and you start to see a finger or thumb twitch)...*"This feeling is building...like your hand wants to move up...I wonder what will happen first?"* (This, by the way, is the classic double bind: it doesn't really matter which hand moves. Either way the subject is succumbing to your suggestions) *"Will your whole hand begin to lift up, or will it be your thumb?...Maybe your index finger...THERE, can you feel your thumb moving?...Can you feel your hand wanting to lift off your leg?...to move up...to rise up in the air...and as it does, you will let it happen...you will not force it to happen, but as it does, you will just allow it to happen..."*

Again, watching for any signs of reaction to your cues, you can feed them back to the subject. *"Your hand is getting very light now...your hand is getting lighter and lighter...wanting to lift up, it's so light, wanting to drift up, d-r-i-f-t u-p...yes...there it is....your hand is floating up...up...u-p...slowly...but moving up...up...up..."*

Once you see movement upward in the hand, you want to plant the following suggestions, by saying, *"As your hand moves up you may begin to feel a force, and invisible force, almost magnetic, that is pulling your fingers apart...your fingers will slowly begin to separate and move apart...you'll notice the spaces between your fingers widen...wider... wider...your fingers are spreading..."* Here you are using the positive response of one suggestion to reinforce another. For instance, an arm rising suggests the fingers want to separate.

Another suggestion is, *"Notice your hand rising in the air...and as it does, the higher it goes, the lighter your arm will get...and as it floats up, you will find your forearm bending at the elbow...your hand will move up, but it will start to move in towards your face...you don't really know exactly where your hand is going, but it is moving in towards your face... moving...floating upward...lighter and lighter as your hand lifts up, and up, and up...your hand is feeling the force of an invisible magnetic attraction to your face...drawn inward...feel the force, almost like some power pushing on your hand...some invisible force drawing your hand in toward your face...upward...into your face...I wonder what part of your face it will touch?...maybe your forehead?...maybe your chin...maybe your nose?...yes, that's it...your nose...your hand is being drawn in towards your nose, and when it touches your nose, something very interesting will happen...when your hand touches your nose, your eyes will close all on their own..."*

Here, we introduce another element. First, the hand lifts up, next fingers separate, then hand moves towards face...and we tie those movements to eyes closing.*"...As soon as your hand touches your nose...your eyes will become so tired and heavy that they will want to close...and you will let them...don't force it to happen, but when it does, just allow it to happen...just allow your eyes to close...you can feel your eyes wanting to close...your hand is getting closer...you can feel your eyes getting tired...you can feel a heaviness in your eyes...your eyelids may want to close...think of nothing else... concentrate...feel your hand being drawn in ...feel the force working...when your hand touches your nose your eyes will close, but your eyes must not close until your hand touches your face...when it does, your eyes will close, and you will drift off into a wonderful state of relation...drift off into a deep, deep sleep...*(again, time your induction speech to what the subject is experiencing)*...it's nearly there...closer...c-l-o-s-e-r... TOUCHING!...eyes wanting to close...your hand you remain in this position...eyes closing...your hand will remain comfortably in this position...eyes closing...eyes closed!..."*

From here, you should go immediately into deepening the hypnotic trance. More on that in a moment. First, let's cover some situations where the subject is *not* responding as we would like.

One technique, if the subject is slow to respond, is to give them something to visualize that will help him channel his thoughts. For example, you might say, *"As your fingers separate, you will feel a lightness come over your hand, as if a balloon is lifting it up in the air...a giant helium balloon on a string, and the string is tied around your wrist...feel the string gently pulling on your wrist* (watching for responses)*...there, it's* *tugging on your wrist, lightly, up...up...up...now TWO balloons are tied to your wrist...two GIANT helium-filled balloons...pulling on your wrist...lifting your hand...and as they rise higher and higher in the air, the balloons are getting bigger and bigger, and as they do, your hand is feeling lighter and lighter...now there are three balloons...four balloons...five...six...SEVEN....EIGHT...NINE...T-E-N GIANT HELIUM-FILLED BALLOONS...your hand is very, very light...lifting up and up..."*

Or, you can try this, *"I want you to imagine that I've attached a big rubber band from the tip of your nose to the back of your hand...feel the rubber band pulling on your hand...feel your hand being drawn in toward your face...*(you might try counting too, to improve the pace of the response)...*as I count to ten, you'll feel the tension in the rubber band pulling more and more on your hand...drawing your hand in towards your face...the rubber band is tightening... one, getting tighter...two, you can feel it pulling...three...pulling your hand in...four...five... drawing your hand inward...six...your hand is being drawn in...seven...eyes getting very sleepy as your hand is being drawn in...eyes getting very heavy, very tired... eight...hand moving in, eyes getting very heavy...and as your hand moves in, the closer it gets to your face, the lighter it feels...the lighter it feels, the move sleepy you feel...hand very light...eyes sleepy...nine...* (pacing the speech to the action of the subject. You don't want the eyes closing before the hand gets to the face, or the hand to get to the face without the eyes getting drowsy. Put the emphasis where it's needed)..*very sleepy...eyes closing...TEN...EYES CLOSED...very good!"*

If you can see that the subject is struggling to want his hand to move, but the movements are painfully slow, or not there at all, give him a start, by gently lift his hand up, saying,*"...and as you concentrate, you will feel your hand rising, like this...wanting to lift, to move, on its own...and as it does, you will let it... "*

Let's just say that the subject's eyes close before his hand reaches his face. In that case say, *"Your eyes have closed, your eyes will remain closed while your hand continues to move in towards your nose...moving faster as you get closer..."*

Say the subject's hand reaches his nose, but he shows no response to the eyes closing suggestion. Here, you might want to say, *"Your hand is touching your nose...eyes getting very tired...sleepy...very sleepy...eyes wanting to close...your hand will remain in this position...eyes closing...*(now take your hand and place it over the person's eyelids and lightly imitate closing them)*...c-l-o-s-i-n-g...c-l-o-s-i-n-g...CLOSED!"* Another approach to this problem is to introduce another aid into the speech, something the person can use to guide your suggestion. One example used above is counting, like we did with the helium balloons. You might want to try this, *"With every breath you take, with every beat of your heart, you will feel your eyes getting strangely heavy...with every breath, with every heart beat, you will feel your eyes growing tired...sleepy...very sleepy...with every breath you take, with every beat of your heart, your eyes will continue to want to close...breathe in deeply...breathe out* (time this to the rising movement of the subject's chest)...*in...out...eyes growing very tired...wanting to close...eyes closing... in...out...eyes c-l-o-s-i-n-g..."*

Or say the subject's hand is not move towards his nose, but towards his chin, repeat, *"...You hand may feel like it wants to move to another part of your face...If it does, let it. Don't force it to happen, but if it does happen, just allow it to happen...SEE!...your hand is being drawn in towards your chin..."*

If the subject's head (or upper body) seems to want to bend forward as his hand is moving in, say, *"...and if your head feels like it wants to move towards your hand...I wonder which one will touch first?...hand moving...head moving..."*

Once the subject's eyes have closed, you should immediately move to deepening the hypnotic state by saying, *"You are now deep asleep...feeling very relaxed, very sleepy...your hand will remain in this position until I say you can lower it...your hand will comfortably remain touching (your nose)...in a moment, you will allow your hand to return to the position it was in when we started, on your lap...as your hand is lowered...AND DON'T ALLOW ANYTHING TO HAPPEN YET...you will find that as your hand descends, the further it goes, the DEEPER and DEEPER you will go into this state of relaxation you're in now...okay, allow your hand to slowly lower...feel your whole body relax...falling deeper and d-e-e-p-e-r into the state of sleep you're in...hand lowering...deeper and deeper to sleep...drifting off deeper and deeper..."* When the hand reaches the lap, say, *"Deep, deep sleep...with every breath you take, with every beat of your heart...you will be drawn deeper and deeper into this wonderful, warm sleep...s-l-e-e-p..."*

A few observations about the method above may be instructive. First, it is very important that you synchronize your speech with the movements of the subject. Second, you cannot stick to the script when the subject is not reacting according to plan Third, you should always watch for any signs or movement from the person that can be incorporated into the induction process.

On this first point, if you are just reading a speech without any synchronizing of the suggestions with actions by the subject, you may create a severe conflict in his mind, one that will block any progress in the induction. You can't blindly read something and expect each person will react the same, or as you command. Tailor your speech to what is happening at that moment.

On point two, if something isn't working, punt! If you're trying to get the person to lift his hand, and his hand isn't lifting, try something else. For example, let's say the subject's hand will not levitate, that for five minutes no reaction is achieved. You might say, *"That was fine. You no longer need to think about your hand rising. Just relax, look up at the object on the wall in front of you..."* and then proceed to the *Eye Fixation* induction technique.

This brings up another point. If something isn't working, make it seem not to matter. Don't make the person too self conscious or nervous that he must "perform" on cue. We're talking about getting into someone's mind. You have to expect the unexpected to happen. Sometimes what happens is nothing, or the wrong thing. Instead of looking at it negatively, try to find a way to use it, to channel it back into your speech in a positive way. Whatever you do, don't make everything a contest, or a win/lose, pass/fail situation. The power to hypnotize is not something you can read off of a piece of paper or memorize and recite. It's gaining a feeling, an empathy, for helping the subject to enter his subconscious mind. As the bus driver on that journey, sometimes you have to go off the beaten path, to explore a highway that will allow *that* person to arrive at *his* inner mind.

This third point, similar to number two, is to use all the positive signals this person is sending you. If his finger is twitching, make it seem as though that's what it's supposed to do and incorporate it into your speech. Don't ignore it.

Repetition in your delivery is also important. You notice that many suggestions are repeated several times. You will find that to strengthen the suggestion, it helps to reinforce the message by saying it over and over.

One last observation. We are using a rather indirect form of hypnosis. When providing the person with suggestions, it's not the person directly who is being asked to do something. Instead of, *"You will make your hand rise up...",* it is, *"Your hand will rise up..."* This way, the person is able to disassociate the movements, to have a lack of responsibility for his action. "It's not *me* making my hand rise. It's my *hand."*

Two Rapid Induction Techniques

If you have ever seen a stage hypnotist perform, that person probably led you to believe that he could hypnotize a subject almost instantly, sometimes by just snapping his fingers (more on this in Chapter 8). While most stage hypnotists are very fast at inducing a trance, most of the reasons have to do with the setting, not the hypnotist. Being on stage gives most people stage fright. What stage hypnotists do is to make you feel that the nervousness you're experiencing is part of the hypnotic experience. They channel your anxiety and tenseness back into something positive.

With great stage presence and style, they make their venue work in their favor. They also have several other factors working for them: subjects typically volunteer, so they *want* to be hypnotized; there is a strong desire to do as the hypnotist tells you, because *you* are part of the "act," and being in a group, you tend to feel *peer pressure.* If the three people before you fall into a deep sleep, you feel more compelled to follow the lead.

Rapid induction techniques work best with subjects who have tested well and exhibit quick responsiveness. As explained before, if you are in the middle of testing a person and they are responding to your suggestions with remarkable ease, you may want to move right into the induction process, using one of the rapid methods described below.

Rapid induction requires you to be more forceful in your approach, more direct, if you will. It will be quite noticeable in the speeches. Here are two methods to try, the *Eye-To-Eye* and *Special Nerve* techniques.

The "Eye-To-Eye" Method

The *Eye-To-Eye* induction technique is not too dissimilar to the methods above, except it employs, as the name says, eye-to-eye contact.

The induction can be performed standing or sitting. Let's assume the subject is seated (I'll describe the standing method after). Position your chair opposite the subject's chair. You should both be seated, with your knees almost touching each other. Sometimes, to get even closer to the subject, you may want to position your knees interlocking his, or to position your chair in such a way that you are in front of, but to the side of the subject, and you each then turn your heads towards one another .

A psychological device to use in this type of situation is to show just how much in command you are, which is very necessary in rapidly inducing hypnosis. You should move the chairs into position, making a big deal out of precisely where they are placed. This gives the subject the feeling you must know what you are doing.

With both of you knee-to-knee, bring your index finger up to your right cheek, under the eye, and say, *"I want you to focus all of your attention on my right eye. I want you to listen only to my words and to focus your attention here."* You should begin to fix a point to stare at somewhere between the subject's nose at the bridge, holding your focus there. Look *through* the subject, rather than *at* him, focusing on an imaginary spot in back of the person's head.

Many times, when asked to look you in the face, the subject will have a hard time not smiling. You should say, *"Relax. It is perfectly okay for you to smile or laugh, since there's nothing serious about what we're about to do, and there should be no reason for you to be frightened or concerned."*

With the person's focus on your eye, and give it five to ten seconds or so before proceeding, repeat, *"When I count to 'three,' I want you to allow your eyes to close...close tightly...You will not go to sleep. You will hear everything I say, and be completely aware of everything that is happening to you. Ready? ...(Wait for response)...One...two...THREE!"...Eyes closing...closing tightly...more tightly closed...they feel as though they are glued shut...you can feel your eyes rolling up in your head...turning upward as though you are looking at a spot near the top of your head...rolling up and back to here* (placing your finger lightly at the middle top part of the person's forehead)...*you can no longer open your eyes. No matter how hard you try, your eyes will NOT open...try opening your eyes...*(allow the person only a second or two to try. Most people, with their eyes rolled back, cannot open their eyelids. It's near impossible to do. This is an example of using a natural physical phenomenon to aid in the induction process.)...*STOP TRYING!...go to sleep...drifting deeper and deeper...d-e-e-p-e-r and d-e-e-p-e-r and d-e-e-p-e-r...very deep!...Feel your head moving down to your chest...feel your whole body grow very relaxed and loose...*(placing your hand on the person's back, slowly ease them down in the chair, head into the chest, if they need help doing so)...*with every breath you take, with every beat of your heart...you will find yourself going deeper and deeper to sleep... drifting deeper and deeper, d-e-e-p-e-r and d-e-e-p-e-r..."* From here you would go into deepening techniques.

Because you are speeding up the induction process, and therefore relying on the subject responding to you almost without hesitation, more negative reaction can occur. Let's go over a couple of these situations, and possible solutions you can use to overcome them.

One negative sign is the subject not looking directly in your eyes, or not holding his stare. Be very forceful and direct in commanding that he do exactly as told.

Another problem that can occur is for the subject to not close his eyes when asked. You can repeat the command a few times, but at some point you need to give the matter added attention. To do this, as you repeat that you want the subject's eyes to close, reach over with your two index fingers and gently extend them in front of his face, just above his eyes, holding them there briefly. Many times this is enough to encourage the eyes to close. You may, however, need to extend your fingers, placing them on the eyelids and close his eyes for him, saying, *"I want your eyes to close now, and remain closed until I tell you otherwise."*

One variation to this induction method is to employ the subject's hands. At the beginning, when seating the person, have them place his hands on his lap, *palms up.* You may want even to take the person's hands in your hand and turn them over. This does a few things. In the palms up position, most people feel a little insecure and helpless. It also affords you the opportunity to test his resistance based on how relaxed his hands are. If his hands are resisting yours, say, *"Just relax and enjoy this experience. All you need to do is listen to my voice and do as I ask".*

The *Eye-To-Eye* technique can also be done with the subject upright. With the subject standing directly in from of you, position yourself so that you are as close as possible to him, about a foot distance between your face and his. You may even want to have one of your feet between the subject's two feet. By "intruding" on the person's "space," you set up a conflict: It makes the subject feel enclosed, or confined, which builds an instant level of anxiety, that you, in turn, can use to channel back into the induction process.

From here, the technique remains pretty much the same. One exception is that you might want to have a chair handy, so that once hypnotized, the subject can be told to sit.

The "Special Nerve" Method

Another rapid induction method, the *Special Nerve* technique, relies on the falsehood that, by touching the subject and hitting certain "nerves," you can produce the emission of magnetic fluids, causing hypnosis, a theory postulated by Mesmer. Believe or not, this works, thanks largely to the fact that few people understand anything about the true origins of hypnosis.

This "theory" needs to be explained to the subject first. *"I don't know if you have ever heard of Franz Mesmer. He was a doctor who, some 200 years ago, discovered what at the time was called 'Animal Magnetism,' what we today call 'Hypnosis.' The word Mesmerized comes from Franz Mesmer. Anyway, this animal magnetism is something in all of us, a 'psychic electricity,' if you will. I'd like to use that force inside you now. Would you like to feel it?"*

With the subject seated as before, go through the following "ritual." Rub your hands together vigorously for ten seconds, then open and close your fingers several times, repeating these two steps twice, or even three times. Extending your hands out, shake them a few times. Next, go through the hand rubbing, and opening and closing of fingers once more, placing your hands on each side of your temple. Finally, close your eyes for five seconds, tilt your head down, appear in deep thought, and then suddenly remove your hands, open your eyes, stare directly at the subject, and say, *"We're ready!"* You then place your left thumb and index finger on the bridge of the person's nose, and the thumb, index, and middle finger at the base of the neck by the shoulder. Initially the two hands should apply moderate, even pressure to these two areas.

"I'm applying pressure to certain nerves in your body, nerves that are directly linked to that part of your brain that controls your conscious mind. By applying pressure to these nerve points, you will begin to feel unusual sensations...you should feel a tingling sensation...as this feeling extends out over your body, you will feel your body begin to relax...you will feel yourself getting very sleepy...with every breath you take, with every beat of your heart, you will feel yourself getting sleepier and s-l-e-e-p-i-e-r...and as I apply more pressure, (press harder) *you will find your eyes are getting very tired...your eyes will be very heavy..."* At this point, the speech is the same as the *Eye-To-Eye* technique.

"When I count to THREE, *I want you to allow your eyes to close...close tightly...You will not go to sleep. You will hear everything I say, and be completely aware of everything that is happening to you. Ready? ...*(Wait for response)*...One...two...THREE!"...Eyes closing...closing tightly...more tightly closed...they feel as though they are glued shut...you can feel your eyes rolling up in your head...turning upward as though you are looking at a spot near the top of your head...rolling up and back to here* (placing your finger lightly at the middle top part of the person's forehead)*...you can no longer open your eyes. No matter how hard you try, your eyes will NOT open...try opening your eyes...*(allow the person only a second or two to try)*...Stop trying!...go to sleep...drifting deeper and deeper...deeper and deeper and deeper...very deep!...Feel your head moving down to your chest...feel your whole body grow very relaxed and loose...*(placing your hand on the person's back, slowly ease them down in the chair if they need help doing so)*...with every breath you take, with every beat of your heart...you will find yourself going deeper and deeper to sleep...drifting deeper and deeper, d-e-e-p-e-r and d-e-e-p-e-r..."*

Ten Rules Of Induction

1. The first rule is that **THERE ARE NO RULES**, and what rules there are, are meant to be broken. As I have said repeatedly, the situation should always dictate the course of action, not the other way around. If it's not working, do something else. Don't worry about sticking to the script.

2. SUCCESS BREEDS SUCCESS. If the subject is responding to something you're saying, use it as a building block to achieve other things. *"Very good! See, your hand is rising, and as it rises, it will get lighter and lighter..."*

3. IF SOMETHING ISN'T WORKING, MAKE IT SEEM NOT TO MATTER. You have to expect the unexpected to happen, and if it does, try to find a way to use it, to channel it back into your speech in a positive way.

4. MAKE YOUR SUGGESTIONS NON-VOLUNTARY. Instead of, *"You will make your hand rise up..."* it is, *"Your hand will rise up..."*

5. THE TONE AND MANNER OF YOUR VOICE ARE VERY IMPORTANT. Any inflections, changes in audible level, pauses, or other features of speech play a big role in how the meaning of words and sentences are interpreted. For example, *"Your arm is stiff and rigid"* versus, *"You arm is STIFF and RIGID. "*

6. <u>CREATE SUGGESTIONS THAT USE AS MANY SENSES AS POSSIBLE</u>. Some people are essentially visual, while others are auditory or tactile (touch). So try to offer suggestions that employ the senses of light, touch, hearing, taste, etc.

7. <u>USE ALL THE POSITIVE SIGNALS YOUR SUBJECT IS SENDING YOU</u>. If his finger is twitching, make it seem as though that's what it's supposed to do, and incorporate it into your speech. Don't ignore it.

8. <u>REPETITION IN YOUR DELIVERY IS VERY IMPORTANT</u>. Any idea that occupies the mind tends to realize itself. You will find that repetition strengthens suggestions, helping to reinforce the message.

9. <u>AVOID AMBIGUITY</u>. Hypnotized people tend to translate your suggestions very literally. Be careful to use suggestions that will not be misinterpreted.

10. <u>DON'T MAKE INDUCTION A CONTEST</u>. It challenges the person to be hypnotized. They'll either think, "I'm too strong to be hypnotized, so just let'em try. I'll resist!" or, "Okay, I'm ready to be hypnotized. When is it going to happen? It's not happening yet...I'm waiting!"

A Footnote To Induction

In theory, every individual is capable of being hypnotized, *under the right conditions and in the proper state of mind.* It is estimated that about one person in five has natural somnambulistic (sleepwalking) tendencies, a condition that closely approaches the spontaneous hypnotic state. For these people, being hypnotized is almost innate. For others, to varying degrees, hypnosis can be induced with careful guidance. The key is having a *motivated* subject.

If you find a subject who, with all your efforts, is not falling into a trance, don't assume your induction techniques to be at fault. Instead, consider reconditioning the subject to be a willing participant in this exercise, even if that means starting the process all over, or canceling the session altogether and rescheduling it. If you don't have a motivated subject, you will not have a hypnotized subject.

Chapter

Deepening Techniques

The subconscious mind believes and accepts without question whatever premise is presented to it. It works with remarkable logic, speed, and lack of criticism.

s I just said, every person can be hypnotized, under the right conditions. And once hypnotized, if left alone, a subject would likely drift from a hypnotic trance to sleep, to wake of his own accord in a few minutes or hours.

While everyone is hypnotizable, each person reaches their own trance level from which it is difficult for them to fall deeper into the hypnotic state. Some people instantly fall into a deep, deep state of hypnosis. Some only experience the very lightest of trances. As a rule, the more often a person is hypnotized, the deeper a trance they can achieve. The reason for wanting the subject to achieve a deepened trace state is that there is a direct correlation between the level of hypnosis and the person's susceptibility to accepting your suggestions. The deeper they are, the more they are functioning through the subconscious mind, the more you are able to do with that individual.

Many scales to judge hypnotic susceptibility exist. Most have 20, 30, 50, even 100 levels. When you simplify it, though, there are really only three levels: light trance; medium trance; and heavy, or somnambulistic (sleep-like) trance.

The signs of a person in a light trance are, in ascending order towards achieving deeper levels: physical relaxation; drowsiness apparent; eyelids fluttering; heaviness of limbs; slower and deeper breathing; aversion to moving, speaking, thinking, or acting; facial twitch; simple posthypnotic suggestions heeded (more on posthypnotic suggestions later); partial feeling of detachment; and recognition of trance (difficult to describe but definitely felt).

Most subjects in a light trance will experience the beginning sensations of hypnosis, but are still heavily in their active conscious state. In this condition, they may find themselves in conflict with their subconscious mind, where the critical factors of reasoning are bypassed, thereby making it difficult on you to have commands readily accepted.

The conscious mind has the ability to do inductive reasoning, whereas the subconscious mind can only use deductive reasoning. In other words, *the subconscious mind believes and accepts without question whatever premise is presented to it. It works with remarkable logic, speed, and lack of criticism.*

By the way, people always ask if a hypnotized subject told to go out and shoot someone will actually do it, ala *The Manchurian Candidate*, or a women told to perform sexual favors will generously comply. *The answer is no* (unless they would do so under non-hypnotized circumstances). The reason is that if you give a suggestion that is morally objectionable to that person, the *critical faculties* of the mind are brought into play, and the suggestion will be rejected.

Kreskin, the well-known mentalist (George Kresge) proved out this theory in a live demonstration. He gave a hypnotized subject orders to leave the stage and after a five-minute delay to return, pick up a butcher knife placed on a table on the stage, and to plunge it into Kreskin's back. The man returned on stage as told, picked up the knife, raised it over Kreskin's back, but then he dropped it and shuddered. The act was contrary to his will, so he refused to carry out the command.

In a medium trance, look for these signs, again in ascending order of deepness: complete muscle inhibitions; partial amnesia; glove anesthesia (more on this later); heightened senses of touch, taste and smell; and a complete catalepsy of limbs or body. In a medium trance, most people are excellent, willing subjects, able to take suggestion well.

In a deep trance, watch for: ability to open eyes without affecting trance; fixed stare with eyes open; somnambulism; complete amnesia; bizarre posthypnotic suggestions heeded; uncontrolled movements of eyes; sensation of floating/out-of-body feeling; rigid muscles; fading sound of your voice; recall of lost memories; age regression (more on this in a later chapter); visual hallucinations; color sensations; stuporous condition in which all spontaneous activity is inhibited. Few subjects, at least initially, can achieve this level. If you can work a subject into a deep trance, the experience, for both you and the person, will be quite exciting!

Regardless of what level a person is in once hypnotized, there are ways to deepen the hypnotic trance, and we're going to explore them now.

Rigid Arm

This is an excellent test of a subject's trance level and, at the same time, a clever way to deepen the hypnotic state.

Taking one of the subject's hands in your hands, holding it by the elbow and the wrist, raise it up parallel with the floor and extend it straight out in front. Before you do, though, let the person know what you're about to do. (As a rule, never touch a subject unless you let them know this in advance, particularly where the subject's eyes are closed) *"In a moment I'm going to take your (right) hand and lift it up. When I do, I want you to give no resistance...*(lifting the hand up)*...I want you to focus all your attention on your arm. As you do, you will notice your arm getting stiff, very stiff...it will become rigid, unable to move...your arm will be locked in place....it's like a steel bar is running through your arm...your arm is as stiff and rigid as a steel bar...AS STIFF AND RIGID AS A STEEL BAR!"*

As you say this, still holding the person's hand, emphasize your words by lightly squeezing the person's arm, *"...STIFF, RIGID...your arm cannot move from this position...it is frozen in this position until I tell you can move it...focus all of your attention on this arm...concentrate on your arm...picture it as STIFF AND RIGID AS A STEEL BAR. In a few moments, I'm going to try to push down on your arm, and as I do, your arm will not move...as hard as I try, your arm will not be able to move...STIFF, RIGID, AS RIGID AS A STEEL BAR...ready? I'm going to press down now* (as you press down)...*you cannot move your arm, stiff and rigid...STIFF AND RIGID...*(after two or three seconds, stop pushing)...

"Okay, I've stopped pushing. Very good! That was excellent. Now in a few moments, I'm going to remove my hand from your arm, and as I do, your arm will IMMEDIATELY fall down to your side, and as it does, it will become very relaxed, very heavy...more relaxed and heavier than before...and you will find that the minute your hand falls down by your side, you will drift off deeper and deeper into the state of relaxation than you're in now...deeper and deeper to sleep...d-e-e-p-e-r and d-e-e-p-e-r...okay, ready? I'm going to count to three, and when I say 'THREE,' I will remove my hands and your arm will immediately drop to your side, and you will drift deeper and deeper to sleep...even deeper and deeper...one...TWO...THREE!! (at the same time quickly removing your hand).

As the person's hand falls by his side, say, *"very relaxed...very sleepy...falling deeper and deeper to sleep...deeper and deeper into a state of relaxation than you're in now..."*

Two ways to judge how deeply under the subject is, can be measured by the rigidity of the arm, that is, how much resistance he puts up, and how quickly and loosely the arm falls by his side when you release it. If you feel only modest resistance, the subject is probably in a light trance. Heavier resistance, a medium trance or deeper. I've seen a 85-pound woman resist a 200-pound man's hand pushing down on her arm. It's amazing how powerful you can become if you focus all your energy on one thing. Remember the story about the mother who lifted the two-ton car off her child?

Watching if the hand collapses at your count, and falls limply by the side, and how fast the hand drops, is another good indication of how deeply the subject is under. It's also a good example of the healing benefits of hypnosis, of how hypnosis can bring profound relaxation to the body, if we channel our energies properly.

The Staircase

This technique involves a visualization method to deepen the hypnotic state. Here, the subject takes a mental trip down a set of stairs. It could just as easily be an elevator or escalator. The idea is to draw a picture in the subject's mind that relates the *physical depth* they imagine to the *hypnotic depth* they are experiencing.

"I want you to picture yourself at the top of a staircase. It's a wide staircase with a railing you can hold on to if you want, or you can imagine holding on to my hand, if it makes you feel better (some subjects will hold out their hands and want to actually hold your hand -- let them). *I'll be with you all the way, so you have nothing to worry about. These are very nice stairs. Can you see the stairs?.....*(look for verbal or non-verbal response)... *Good. You will notice that there are ten steps leading down to the landing below. Go ahead, count them yourself, count the ten steps. When you've finished*

counting them let me know by nodding your head...(look for response)...*Do you see the landing, too...*(look for response)...*Very good."*

"Now in a few moments, we are going to slowing take a walk down these stairs, and as we do, you will notice that with every step we take, you will become more and more relaxed...that with each step, you will fall deeper and deeper into this state of relaxation that you're in now...ready?...We're taking that first step...becoming more relaxed...second step...going deeper and deeper to sleep...the third step, still deeper...the fourth step...getting very, very relaxed...the fifth step, we're half way down the steps....going down deeper and deeper, feeling better and better...the six step...the seventh step...DEEP...DEEPER...VERY DEEP SLEEP...the eight step, almost at the bottom, deeper still...the ninth step..."

You can end the deepening exercise here, or, if the subject is responding well and you want to continue, you can add, *"One more step, one step to the landing. Before we take that step, I want you to look over to the side of the landing...look, there's another set of identical steps...ten more steps...let's take the next step to the landing...good, we've reached the landing now, and are ready to descend the other steps...one...d-e-e-p-e-r...two, still deeper... three... four...very relaxed....feeling very good...five... down... down... down...six... seven, d-e-e-p-e-r and d-e-e-p-e-r...almost at the bottom...nine...one more step...ten...excellent!"*

Head Down

This deepening technique is something you can do at any time, particularly when the subject is first hypnotized. Normally when a person is entering a hypnotized state, you will see his head fall down, an upward rolling of the eyes into his head, his arms go limp, his breathing will become heavier and more pronounced, and his pulse will quicken (damp, warm hands, a common sign, indicate a nervousness on the subject's part, and cold, dry hands are a sign of the subject is resisting you). At this point, say, *"You are feeling very good...very sleepy...In a moment I'm going to place my hands on your shoulders, and as I do, you will feel a downward pressure as I lower your body...And as I do, you will feel yourself going deeper and deeper into this state of relaxation...deeper and deeper...don't worry about falling out of the chair...you will not fall out of the chair...just allow yourself to relax, to go deeper and deeper* (keep a gentle pressure on the back, lowering the person's chest to the waist as his resistance drops)...*deeper and deeper...and d-e-e-p-e-r...drifting off into a wonderful s-l-e-e-p..."*

Awaken And Go Deeper

Using the *Head Down* technique, you can move right into one of the best methods for deepening the hypnotic state: to wake the person and then return them to the hypnotic state again. If done right, it can produce dramatic results. The one danger is that, if the subject is only in a very light trance, they may wake, only to come out of the trance. Be certain, then, that the subject is at least in an advanced stage of light trance before attempting this.

"You are very relaxed, feeling very good...In a few moments, I'm going to wake you, and when I do, you will feel refreshed, renewed, full of energy...feeling wonderful

about yourself and everything that's happened to you...To do this, to waken you, I will count to ten, and by the time I reach 'ten,' and say the word 'AWAKE!,' you will be wide awake. Again, I will count to ten, say 'AWAKE,' and you will be wide awake, you will immediately open your eyes, you will sit up in your chair, feeling exactly the same as you do when you wake up in the morning after a good night's sleep....And, anytime I want you to go back to this sleep, to the state of relaxation you're in now, all I will do is SNAP MY FINGERS and say the word 'SLEEP!', and you will INSTANTLY CLOSE YOU EYES and drift off into this sleep...In fact, when I say the word 'SLEEP,' you will drift off into a sleep much, MUCH deeper than the one you're in now, you will fade into a d-e-e-p, d-e-e-p, D-E-E-P S-L-E-E-P...Do you understand the instructions I've given you? If you do nod your head...(wait for response)...very good. Again, I'll count to ten, and then say the word 'awake!,' and you will open your eyes and be wide awake, remembering everything that's taken place so far today...and anytime I say the word 'SLEEP,' and snap my fingers you will IMMEDIATELY close your eyes and drift off into a sleep even deeper than the one you're in now...Ready? Nod if you are...(look for response)... okay, here we go...one you're sleeping deeply, but now it's time to get up...two... beginning to wake up...three...four...feeling very good...five...six...waken up more....seven...eight...waking...NINE...TEN...(snapping your finger) AWAKE!"

The subject should be wide awake, eyes open, sitting up. If not, say, *"You're wide awake now, you can open your eyes...eyes opening...AWAKE!"* Talk to the subject now about how they felt under hypnosis, *"Do you remember what just happen? Are you enjoying the experience so far? What does it feel like?"*

In the middle of answering one of your questions, when the person is looking you right in the eye (if not, position yourself so that he is, or tell him to look you in the eye when responding), right as he is mid-sentence, snap your finger and say, *"SLEEP!"* The subject should almost instantly do as you've told him to do. If not, immediately snap your finger again, and repeat, *"SLEEP."* If you need you, or if you want to add a bit of drama, as you snap your finger and say, *" SLEEP,"* take your hand and place it over the person's eyelids and lightly imitate closing them, and as the person does, reach in back and place a hand on his back and slowly pull him down in his chair so that his chest is in his lap.

As soon as the person's eyes close, say, *"Drifting deeper and deeper to sleep, deeper and deeper into this state of relaxation...with every breath you take, with every beat of your heart, you will find yourself drifting d-e-e-p-e-r, and d-e-e-p-e-r, and d-e-e-p-e-r..."*

After a few moments of this, you want to wake the subject again. *"In a moment, I'm going to wake you again, and just as before, I will count to ten, say the word 'AWAKE,' you will instantly be awake, open your eyes, feeling refreshed, and renewed...Ready? (wait for a response) one...two...three, waking...four...five...six...feeling very good...seven...eight...nine, almost awake... TEN, AWAKE!"*

What is happening here is that, first, you are conditioning the person to respond on cue to your commands. This will be important later on. And second, you are allowing that person a pathway, if you will, to channel his mind deeper into the subconscious.

Once you've woken up the subject, go through the same questioning routine, and once more, in the middle of it, put him back to sleep. Asleep again, give this new command, *"You're doing quite well, you're feeling very good. In a moment I'm going to wake you up again, but this time when I do, I want you to get up from your chair, walk across the room to (the table over in the corner, or another object in the room), turn around and return to the chair you're sitting in now, and THE MOMENT YOU ARE SEATED AGAIN, without me saying a word, you will IMMEDIATELY close your eyes, drifting deeper and deeper to sleep, deeper and deeper into this state of relaxation...with every breath you take, with every beat of your heart, you will find yourself drifting d-e-e-p-e-r, and d-e-e-p-e-r, and d-e-e-p-e-r..."*

This deepening process, of waking the person and putting him back to sleep, can be continued an unlimited number of times. Ideally though, two or three times is more than enough, and it's really based more on the results you're seeing. If the subject is able to go deeper and deeper into the trance with each awake/sleep session, you may wish to continue it.

Forget Your Name

Here's a deepening technique that's humorous, too. In putting the subject repeatedly through the process of awakening, sleeping, deepening, we are attempting to bring that person into a progressively deeper and deeper trance state. At some point, as he begins to enter the mid-levels of a trance, the subject will be susceptible to experiencing partial amnesia. Here's a good way to test for that level, and, at the same time, deepen the trance.

Let's assume that you have awakened and "re-hypnotized" the subject a few times, each time he gets successively deeper, to the point where you feel he is in a mid-level trance. Try this suggestion: *"When you wake, and until I tell you otherwise, you will not be able to remember your last name. As hard as you try, you will not be able to say your last name. You'll remember your first name, but you will not be able to remember your last name. And when you wake, and until I tell you otherwise, you will not remember that I gave you these instructions...do you understand?* (look for a response)...*Again, when I wake you, you will not be able to say your last name, and you will not remember that I gave you these instructions..."*

When you wake the subject, at some point in questioning him, maybe first asking about how he feels and if he is enjoying himself, you might ask some innocuous question like, *"What day is it today?"* After a few simple questions, almost as a casual act, say, *"Oh, by the way Bill, what did you say your last name was?"* Subjects in this situation usually become very puzzled and experience a blank expression on their faces. Some become flush and visibly nervous. You will see them struggling to find their last name. Don't let them go on too long. Quickly brush off the question by asking another question, *" Okay, forget that question. Let me ask you about something else. Tell me what you do for a living,"* or say, *"SLEEP!"* and put the person back to sleep.

Once asleep, work on deepening the person, using methods described earlier. Then, when you are ready to wake the subject again, try this suggestion: *"This time when you wake, and until I tell you otherwise, you will not be able to remember your <u>first</u> name. As hard as you try, you will not be able to say your <u>first</u> name. You'll remember your last name, but you will not be able to remember your first name. And when you wake, and until I tell you otherwise, you will not remember that I gave you these instructions...do you understand?* (look for a response)...*Again, when I wake you, you* *will not be able to remember your first name, and you will not remember that I gave you these instructions..."*

Naturally, when he wakes, you go through the same type of routine as described above, and when you ask what his first name is, the perplexed, blank stare reappears. Now we're having fun! This person is really confused. First he couldn't remember his last name. Now he can't remember his first name. And he's not sure why.

You can continue this routine indefinitely, or introduce other elements: forgetting his birth date, someone else's name, or a number, like the number "4". *"When you wake, and until I tell you otherwise, you will not be able to remember the number four, as soon as you awaken and pick up your head, the number four will drop right out of your mind...it will be completely gone....and you will not be able to find the number four anymore...unless I tell you otherwise...As hard as you try, you will not be able to remember the number four. You'll remember all the other numbers, like one, two, three, five, six...seven, eight, nine, ten, but you will not be able to find the number four. And when you wake, and until I tell you otherwise, you will not remember that I gave you these instructions...do you understand?* (look for a response)...*Again, when I waken you, you will not be able to remember the number four, and you will not remember that I gave you these instructions..."*

When you wake the subject, at some point in questioning him ask, *"I wonder if you could help me in a little experiment? ...Good, could you just count from one to ten for me?"* Again, subjects in this situation usually become very embarrassed as they struggle to find the missing number. To build on the opportunity, say, *"Okay, forget that question. Let me ask this: How much is two plus two?"* You thought they were confused before? Boy, are they confused now!

Here are two more variations on this theme. Tell the person that whenever you ask him his name, he is to respond, *"Elvis!"* or whatever crazy name you can think of, like *Rumplestiltskin.* Another thing to do is tie two events together. For instance, any time the subject is asked what his first name is he can't remember. But, if you say the word, *"Horseradish,"* it will instantly come back to him, *except,* now he will forget his *last* name.

While this is great fun, it is also a good way to deepen the trance. It plays off beautifully on the confusion created, and the realization of the "power" you possess over him.

The Five Rules For Deepening

1. The first rule, as in *all* aspects of hypnosis, is that **THERE ARE NO RULES**, and what rules there are, are meant to be broken. I can't stress enough, if it's not working, do something else.

2. GIVE ONLY ONE SUGGESTION AT A TIME. Too many suggestions at once may cause confusion. Try to work on one at a time, until accepted, and then use it as a building block to the next suggestion.

3. WORK AT THE SUBJECT'S PACE. The person should be allowed to deepen the trance at his own pace. Don't push the process too hard when the situation doesn't warrant it. The more complex the suggestion, the more time you need to give the subject to orient himself to what is expected.

4. BE CAREFUL OF DIRECT CHALLENGES. If you say, *"Your eyes will not open,"* and the subject's eyes do, you have a major setback on your hands. Try a more permissive approach, like, *"You know you can open your eyes if you want to, but it feels so good not to, that to do so would disturb the state of relaxation that you're in now, and therefore, when I ask you to try and open your eyes, they will not open".*

5. ALWAYS BE DEEPENING. Once hypnotized, most subjects will, if left alone, drift upward and away from their trance state. Always try to incorporate deepening techniques into everything you do.

Hypnotic Routines You Can Perform

"What you'll notice is that Tom's NOSE is very sexy...I'm talking very, very sensual, it will be so exciting to look at it that you'll have a hard time NOT staring at Tom's nose...and if he starts RUBBING his nose...OH BOY, WILL YOU GET EXCITED...and the FASTER he rubs his nose...the more aroused you'll become...."

Having hypnotized your subject, what you probably have on your hands is a person very relaxed in his chair, head leaning on the chest, breathing deeply, and looking very much asleep. Except he is definitely *not* asleep. He is in his subconscious mind, ready, willing, and able to accept your suggestions.

Here are some interesting and fun things you can do. Let's start with some easy-to-do routines, and work up to the bigger stuff.

Stuck Like Glue

Here's a good place to start. With the subject seated, say, *"In a minute I'm going to wake you up, and when I do, and until I tell you otherwise, you will be stuck to your chair, unable to get up from your seat...In all other respects, you will feel fine and perfectly normal, except it will be as though you are GLUED to your chair...and the harder you try, the MORE you will be stuck to the seat...no matter how hard you try, YOU WILL NOT BE ABLE TO GET OUT OF THE CHAIR...and after you wake, you will be unaware I have told you this, and you will be unaware that you cannot get out of your chair...and unaware of my telling you this now."*

Using the awaking procedure used earlier, *"I'm going to wake you now, and when I do, you will feel refreshed, renewed, full of energy...feeling wonderful about yourself and everything that's happened to you...I will count to ten, and by the time I reach 'ten,' and say the word 'AWAKE!,' you will be wide wake, you will immediately open your eyes, you will sit up in your chair, feeling exactly the same as you do when you wake up in the morning after a good night's sleep....And, when you wake and until I tell you otherwise, you will be stuck to your chair, unable to get up from your seat...*

*"In all other respects, you will feel fine and perfectly normal, except it will be as though you are GLUED to your chair...and the harder you try, the MORE you will be stuck to the seat...no matter how hard you try, YOU WILL NOT BE ABLE TO GET OUT OF THE CHAIR...and after you wake, you will be unaware I have told you this, and you will be unaware that you cannot get out of your chair...and of my telling you this now...Anytime I want you to go back to this sleep, to the state of relaxation you're in now, all I will do is SNAP MY FINGERS and say the word 'SLEEP!', and you will INSTANTLY CLOSE YOUR EYES and drift off into this sleep...In fact, when I say the word 'SLEEP,' you will drift off into a sleep much, much deeper than the one you're in now, you will fade into a d-e-e-p, d-e-e-p, D-E-E-P S-L-E-E-P...Do you understand the instructions I've given you? If you do nod your head...(wait for response)...very good...okay, here we go...one...two... three...four, starting to wake...five...six...waking up more....seven...eight...waking...NINE...TEN... (*snapping your finger) AWAKE!"*

The subject should be wide awake, eyes open, sitting up. *"Bill, how do you feel?...(*wait for a response)...*Listen Bill, could you do me a favor and go over there* (pointing to the other end of the room or some place outside the room) *and get me (that book, object, glass of water, etc.)..."*

As Bill struggles to get up from the chair, uncertain as to why he can't remove himself from the seat, say, *"Bill, come on, all I want you to do is walk over there and get me (the object requested)...can't you do THAT for ME?"* Some people become so frustrated over the feeling, that they literally pick up the chair by both hands and walk it and themselves over to the object. Before he gets too confused, though, put him back to sleep. Getting the subjects attention, looking him in the face, say *"Bill, SLEEP! (*snapping your fingers)."*

This time when he awakes, you might want to add in a new wrinkle: his hands get stuck, too. *"Bill, in a minute I'm going to wake you up again, just like before, but when I do, and until I tell you otherwise, you will not only be stuck to your chair, unable to get up from your seat, if either or both of your hands touch the sides of your chair, you will find that they, too, instantly stick to that spot, unable to be removed, until I tell you otherwise...It will be as though you are glued to your chair and, if your hands touch the chair, your hands are glued to the chair also...and the harder you try, the more they will be stuck to the chair...no matter how hard you try, YOU WILL NOT BE ABLE TO GET OUT OF THE SEAT OR TO REMOVE YOUR HANDS FROM THE CHAIR...and after you wake, you will be unaware I have told you this, and you will be unaware that you cannot get out of your chair...and of my telling you this now."*

Using the awakening procedure above, wake the subject. Start out with a few easy questions. *"Bill, how do you feel?"* Then ask, *"Could you just get up and change chairs with me please?"* As he struggles to get up, he may try to use his hands to push himself out of the chair, if he does, his hands should stick to the seat. Or, you may want to suggest, *"Bill, can't you get up? Use your hands! Push yourself out of the chair!"*

You can stretch this routine out for some time, or, after trying for a few seconds, you can introduce another element. Placing the subject back to sleep, tell him that when he wakes, he will still be stuck in the chair, but his hands will be free, *until he either puts a hand on his head or in his shirt or pants pocket.* If he does either or both of these things, he will find his hand instantly will be stuck.

"Bill, in a few seconds I'm going to wake you up again, just like before, when I do, and until I tell you otherwise, you will still be stuck to your chair, unable to get up from your seat, BUT YOUR HANDS WILL NO LONGER BE STUCK TO THE SIDES OF YOUR CHAIR...you will be able to freely move them, BUT, if one of your hands touches your HEAD, it will be instantly stuck in this position...you will not be able to remove it until I tell you otherwise ...and if you place either of your hands in your shirt or pants POCKET, that hand will instantly be stuck in the pocket, unable to be removed until I tell you otherwise...It will be as though you are glued to your chair and, if either of your hands touch your head or are placed in your pocket, your hands will be glued in place...and the harder you try, the more you will be stuck to the chair and your hands stuck in place...no matter how hard you try, YOU WILL NOT BE ABLE TO GET OUT OF THE SEAT OR TO UNSTICK YOUR HANDS ..and after you wake, you will be unaware I have told you this, and you will be unaware that you cannot get out of your chair...you will be unaware that your hands will instantly stick if you touch your head or put a hand in your pocket...and you will be unaware of my telling you this now."

There are all kinds of amusing things you can do. Asking him to reach into his pocket to get something, telling him there's a small bird nesting on top of his head, and on and on. You get the idea!

One more variation to this routine is to say at the beginning, *"When I wake you, and until I tell you otherwise, you will be stuck to your chair, unable to get up from your seat...Unless you hear me say 'fried egg' (or any word you choose)...If I say 'fried egg,' you will immediately be able to get up...and when I say 'fried egg,' you will notice that your chair will start to heat up...it will be as though you are sitting on an electric heater and someone turned the switch on...in a few seconds it will get quite hot and you have to practically jump out of your chair, it will get THAT HOT!... Again, when you wake up, in all other respects, you will feel fine and perfectly normal, except it will be as though you are GLUED to your chair...and the harder you try, the MORE you will be stuck to the seat...no matter how hard you try, YOU WILL NOT BE ABLE TO GET OUT OF THE CHAIR...but if I say 'fried egg,' you will instantly be able to get up from your seat, and your chair will start to heat up, to the point that in a few seconds it will get so unbearably hot, you'll LEAP from your chair...and after you wake, you will be unaware I have told you this, and you will be unaware that you cannot get out of your chair...and of my telling you this now."*

Upon waking the subject, go through the normal routine, except let the secret word creep into the conversation, *"Bill, you're acting like a guy eating a fried egg..."* Watch his reaction! By the way, if he doesn't react as expected, he may have missed his "cue," so repeat the sentence. That usually does it.

When you want to move on to other routines, remember this important rule: having completed one series, always remove the suggestion by telling the subject to forget what you just said, and to sleep. Do this before presenting any new set of suggestions, or one might conflict with the other. I can't stress this enough. Let's say, for instance, you've completed this routine and are ready to move on to another. With the subject asleep (it can be done in the waking state, too), say, *"Bill, your hands are now unstuck, you are no longer glued to the chair, you can freely move your hands and you can get up from the chair without any problems whatsoever, and your chair is not hot."*

Magic X-Ray Vision

Here's something that adds spice to the routine and is great to use at parties, because you should have a crowd in the room, at least two or three other people, and the more the merrier.

Fashion an "X-Ray Eye" out of a piece of heavy black cardboard, about three inches square, with a one inch hole cut out of the center. You might want to make a few if you plan to do this in a group and several people will be participating (see Stage Hypnotism, Chapter 8). If you're working more impromptu, and didn't bring your X-Ray Eye, any pair of regular glasses will do.

The routine starts out something like this, *"In a minute, I'm going to wake you, before I do, though, I want to give you something...it's my own invention...I call it my 'X-RAY EYE'...it can do amazing things, as you're about to discover* (handing the eye to the subject)...*Now let me tell you something about the object you hold in your hand...I call it my X-Ray Eye because, when you look through the hole in the middle of it, you can see through clothing...that's right, you can see right through peoples' clothing... and, you know what else is great? No one will know you can see them naked....ISN'T THAT GREAT?* (watch for response)...*Don't do anything with your X-Ray Eye yet...let me tell you more...Like I said, when you look through the eye, you will be able to see people naked...they won't know you can see them naked...that will be fun...Now, there are two other things you need to know...The first is that I'm wearing special protective clothing and you won't be able to see ME naked...The second is that if I catch you looking through the X-Ray Eye, I'm going to have to take it away from you...So if you see me looking at you, HIDE THE X-RAY EYE...Again, you will see able to see everyone but me naked...and if I catch you looking at anyone, I have to take your X-Ray Eye away...Make sure you keep it hidden...You might want to put the hand you have it in now behind your back, so no one can see it...*

"...Okay, I'm about to wake you up...Do you understand how the X-Ray Eye works? (wait for response)...*Good, once more, you can't let me catch you using the X-Ray Eye, so hide it in your hand or somewhere else whenever I look your way...otherwise, you're free to stare at anyone you want...finally, after you wake, you will be unaware I have told you all of this, and of my telling you this now...*

"...I'm going to wake you now, and when I do, you will feel refreshed, renewed, full of energy...feeling wonderful about yourself and everything that's happened to you...I will count to ten, and by the time I reach 'ten,' and say the word 'AWAKE!,' you will be wide wake, you will immediately open your eyes, you will sit up in your chair, feeling exactly the same as you do when you wake up in the morning after a good night's sleep....And, anytime I want you to go back to this sleep, to the state of relaxation you're in now, all I will do is SNAP MY FINGERS and say the word 'SLEEP!',' and you will INSTANTLY CLOSE YOUR EYES and drift off into this sleep...In fact, when I say the word 'SLEEP,' you will drift off into a sleep much, much deeper than the one you're in now, you will fade into a d-e-e-p, d-e-e-p, D-E-E-P S-L-E-E-P ...Do you understand the instructions I've given you? If you do nod your head...(wait for response)...*very good...okay, here we go...one...two... three... four, starting to wake...five... six...waking up more....seven... eight...waking... NINE... TEN...(snapping your finger) AWAKE!"*

With the subject awake, *"Listen Bill, I need to talk to* (Sally, Bob, Mary, etc.) *over here for a minute* (or make up any excuse to turn away from the subject)." While you do this, the subject has probably taken out the Eye and is staring intently, trying to survey the whole room. This usually causes snickers and even laughter among the group. The subject probably has a big grin on his face, too.

Give the person five to ten seconds, pretending you're talking to someone else or distracted by something happening away from the subject, then, announce, *"HEY, WHAT'S GOING ON?"* (to give him time to hide the Eye again) then whirl around and say, *"Bill, is there something going on around here?"* You'll normally get a sheepish response, as the subject guiltily says something dumb like, "Nothing..." Act like you'll accept the answer, but you're a little skeptical.

On some other pretext, turn your back to the subject once more. *"Now Bill, don't interrupt me again. I was in the middle of* (whatever your excuse was)..." You can expect he'll whip out the Eye again. The noise and laughter of the crowd will tip you off. When it happens, go through the same bit again, allowing him time to palm the Eye, and pretending to miss what's going on.

Once more, fake an excuse, turning your back. When the action starts, say, *"Bill, you better not be using one of those X-Ray Eyes that I've heard about. If you are, I'll have to take it away from you!"* Boy, will he hide that Eye, and *fast*.

You can continue this indefinitely, but when you're ready to move on to the next routine, remember to remove the suggestion. Back in the sleep state, repeat, *"Bill, your magic X-Ray Eye has lost its ability. You can no longer look through clothing with it. It's now just a piece of cardboard with a hole in the middle."*

One variation on this routine, is to suggest to the subject that when you say the word, *"Ketchup"* (or any word you choose), the X-Ray Eye will no longer work, *but that everyone else in the room will have instant X-Ray vision, and be able to see HIM naked.* The suggestion can be given at the very beginning, or added later (requiring you put the person back to sleep).

Here's how to do that. Say, for instance, you've just turned back around, hearing all the commotion, *"Did you just hide something behind your back?"* He will most likely deny it, and in the middle of his answer, you snap your fingers and say, *SLEEP!"* With the subject asleep, give the suggestion, *"Bill, when I wake you, you will continue to be able to use your X-Ray Eye, but if you hear me say the word 'KETCHUP,' your magic X-Ray Eye will no longer work, What will happen though, is that everyone in the room will be able to see YOU NAKED...remember, when I say 'Ketchup,' your X-Ray Eye will no longer work and everyone else will be able to see through YOUR clothes...after you wake, you will be unaware I have told you all of this, and of my telling you this now...*

"...I'm going to wake you now...here we go...one...two... three...four, starting to wake...five... six...waking up more....seven...eight...waking...NINE... TEN...(snapping your finger) AWAKE!" When the subject wakes up, you can start back in with the same routine, and at some point, work the special word, in this case, *"Ketchup,"* into the conversation. Make sure everyone is in on the joke, and ready to pretend to have X-ray vision when the time comes.

"Bill, I'm going to give you one more chance...I have to talk with ___, so be on your best behavior for the next minute." After the crowd starts up again, say, *"Bill, you better not have an X-Ray Eye, or so help me...(you slowly turn)...I'll ...I'll...hey, what's that you're hiding (pointing)(behind your back, in your hand, etc.)?...Is it 'KETCHUP'?"* Now watch what happens! The crowd goes into its routine, and starts staring at the subject, pointing, giggling, laughing, whispering to each other. Meanwhile, this poor guy, is covering up and looking for a place to hide! Be sure to end the routine before things get too far out of hand. *"Bill, (snapping your finger) SLEEP!...Deep SLEEP, drifting off deeper and deeper. to sleep Bill, everything is back to normal...No one has X-Ray vision...no one can see through your clothes, and you can't see through anyone else's either."*

A word of caution is in order. Anytime you're performing routines like *Magic X-Ray Vision,* that can potentially embarrass someone, even though they may be innocent and very funny to everyone else, you have to use some discretion, and know when and when not a routine is appropriate, and who will be a good sport, and who may likely find it very offensive, or worse, traumatic.

A good rule, under all circumstances is at the beginning, before you attempt to hypnotize anyone, to say, *"Everything we're going to do tonight (today, this afternoon, etc.) is for FUN. Everyone here wants to enjoy themselves. Whatever you do, whatever happens is all in fun. The entire evening (afternoon, etc.) is all for FUN. You, right along with everyone else, will have a wonderful time and have plenty of fun."*

Who Nose What Turns You On

If you've got an adult crowd, you might try this one with a willing female participant. With the subject asleep, say, *"In a minute I'm going to waken you,...and when I do, you will notice something different about Tom* (or any male in the room. You'll need to clue this person in on what to do) *...something he has always had, but you may not have noticed...what you'll notice is that Tom's NOSE is very sexy...I don't mean just attractive, I mean S-E-X-Y, I'm talking very, very sensual, it will be so exciting to look at it that you'll have a hard time NOT staring at Tom's nose...and if he starts RUBBING his nose...OH BOY, WILL YOU GET EXCITED...it will be a real turn on!...and the MORE he rubs his nose, and the FASTER he rubs his nose...the more aroused you'll become...AND WHAT'S GREAT IS THAT NO ONE WILL NOTICE...YOU CAN GET AS EXCITED AS YOU WANT AND NO ONE WILL BE ABLE TO TELL...and the more Tom continues to rub his nose, the more it will drive you crazy... finally, after you wake, you will be unaware I have told you all of this, and of my telling you this now...*

"...I'm going to wake you now, and when I do, you will feel refreshed, renewed, full of energy...feeling wonderful about yourself and everything that's happened to you...I will count to ten, and by the time I reach 'ten,' and say the word 'AWAKE!,' you will be wide wake, you will immediately open your eyes, you will sit up in your chair, feeling exactly the same as you do when you wake up in the morning after a good night's sleep....And, anytime I want you to go back to this sleep, to the state of relaxation you're in now, all I will do IS SNAP MY FINGERS and say the word 'SLEEP,' and you will INSTANTLY CLOSE YOUR EYES, and drift off into this sleep...In fact, when I say the word 'SLEEP,' you will drift off into a sleep much, much deeper than the one you're in now, you will fade into a d-e-e-p, d-e-e-p, D-E-E-P S-L-E-E-P.

"Remember, the more Tom rubs his nose, and the faster he rubs his nose...the more aroused you'll become...no one will notice...you can get as excited as you want and no one will be able to tell...finally, after you wake, you will be unaware I have told you all of this, and of my telling you this now...Do you understand the instructions I've given you? If you do nod your head...(wait for response)...very good...okay, here we go...one... two... three... four, starting to wake...five...six...waking up more...seven...eight...waking... NINE...TEN... (snapping your fingers) AWAKE!"

(Let's call our subject "Mary") *"Mary, how do you feel?...(after some small talk)...Listen Mary, if you don't mind, I'd like to ask Tom a few questions. Is that okay?...(waiting for her approval, you then turn to Tom)...Tom, what do you think of Mary, isn't she doing great?..."* Tom, who's in on the routine, begins to answer something about how good a subject she is, and as he does, he begins to rub his nose, just lightly at first, but steadily.

Our subject should be reacting to Tom's rubbing. If she is, say, *"Mary, you look like you're enjoying yourself, too...are you enjoying yourself now?"* Mary will probably have a grin on her face, and answer in the affirmative.

To add even more excitement to the routine (and to Mary), after a few minutes of this, put her back to sleep, *"SLEEP MARY!* (snapping your finger) and give her this new suggestion. *"Mary...I'm going to wake you again, and this time when I do, just like before, the more Tom rubs his nose, and the faster he rubs his nose...the more aroused you'll become...no one will notice...you can get as excited as you want and no one will be able to tell...and as you get excited, the more excited you become, the more you will have an uncontrollable urge to HUM...as you become more and more aroused, you will hum out loud...and the more you become excited, the more you will hum...and THE MORE YOU HUM, THE MORE EXCITED YOU WILL GET...you will find that you get very excited by humming...finally, after you wake, you will be unaware I have told you all of this, and of my telling you this now...Do you understand the instructions I've given you? If you do, nod your head...(wait for response)...very good...okay, here we go...one...two... three...four, starting to wake...five... six...waking up more....seven... eight... waking...NINE... TEN...(snapping your finger) AWAKE!"*

This time when you wake the subject, continue the line of questioning, going back and forth between our subject and our accomplice. For example, *"Tom, Mary seems to be enjoying herself, doesn't she?...Mary, you seem a little fidgety, is everything okay?....(as she starts to hum)...Tom, is there something different about you today?* (He shakes his head and says, "No".)*...I'd swear there's something ...is it?...no...it's your face...That's it!...you changed something...your mustache...no, your hair?...no...your NOSE...that's it!...your nose is different, isn't it?* (again, Tom denies it)*...Mary, do you notice anything different about Tom's nose?..."* She should be speaking and humming like a kid trying to answer her parent that she's not eating candy when she's got the whole box in her mouth!

We can't stop here! Let's introduce one more element, putting the subject back to sleep, *"SLEEP MARY!"* (snapping your finger) you give her this suggestion. *"Mary...I'm going to wake you once more, and this time when I do, just like before, the more Tom rubs his nose, and the faster he rubs his nose...the more aroused you'll become...no one will notice...you can get as excited as you want and no one will be able to tell...and as you get excited, the more excited you become, the more you will have an uncontrollable urge to hum...as you become more and more aroused, you will hum out loud...and the more you become excited, the more you will hum...the more you hum, the more excited you will get...and one more thing...If Tom says 'DING-DONG,' you will find that the word DING-DONG really turns you on even more...and as Tom says DING-DONG, each time he does, it will make you go wild ...to the point that you'll have an uncontrollable urge to get up from your chair and go to Tom and passionately squeeze his body...THAT'S HOW GREAT THE FEELING WILL BE...if Tom rubs his nose, you will get excited, the faster he rubs his nose...the more excited you'll become...no one will notice...you can get as excited as you want and no one will be able to tell...and the more excited you become, the more you will have an uncontrollable urge to hum...the more you hum, the more excited you will get...and if Tom says 'DING-DONG,' you will find that the word DING-DONG really turns you on even more...and as Tom says DING-DONG, each time he does, it will make you go wild ...to the point where you'll have an uncontrollable urge to get up from your chair and go to Tom and attack his body...Finally, after you wake, you will be unaware I have told you all of this, and of my telling you this now...Do you understand the instructions I've given you? If you do nod your head...(wait for response)...very good...okay, here we go...one...two... three...four, starting to wake...five... six...waking up more....seven... eight...waking...NINE... TEN...(snapping your finger) AWAKE!"*

Like all the routines, this one can go on forever. With the introduction of this new element, you might want to build to it, asking more innocent questions, working up to stuff like, *"So Tom, I understand you just did some work around your house. What kind of work?",* and he replies, "I fixed the front door bell, *DING DONG!"* *"Tom, you said you fixed what?"* "DING DONG, DING DONG!" Turning to Mary, *"Mary, Tom's a real Mister Fixit, wouldn't you say?...Do you like men who are handy with their noses...ah, I mean handy around the house?* Turning to Tom, who says, "All I have to say is DING DONG, DING DONG, DING DONG..." Anyway, you get the idea.

When Mary does get up to run over to Tom, give her the cue, *"SLEEP!"* and the visual hand signal (snap fingers) just as she's about to reach him. Be sure to say it plenty loud. This will make for a grand finish to the routine.

A Half Dozen More Hypnotic Routines

1. FINGERS STUCK

Tell a subject, *"Place your finger tips together, like this...and as you do, you will find that they are getting stuck together...tighter and tighter...they are glued to one another...your fingers are stuck together...tight...tight... tighter....you cannot pull them apart, no matter how hard to try...they are glued together...try to pull them apart!..."* After struggling with the fingers for a few seconds say, *"All right, stop trying to separate your fingers...relax...forget about your fingers..they will come apart now."*

2. SHAKY HANDS

Hand a subject a glass of water and tell him, *"No matter how hard you try, you will not be able to drink this water...every time you start to drink... your hands will shake, and the water will spill all over you...and the harder you try, the more your hands will shake..."*

3. FINGERS IN THE EARS

Tell a subject to place his index fingers in his ears, then say, *"No matter how hard you try, you will not be able to remove your fingers from your ears...try as you might...you cannot remove your fingers from your ears."*

4. SO YOU WANT TO BE IN *SHOE* BUSINESS?

Tell a subject that his shoes are hurting because he has them on backwards and to switch the left shoe for the right foot, and visa versa. Then, when he's done that, tell him that his shoes feel comfortable, and he should walk around and try them out.

5. YOU THINK YOU'RE STRONG, HUH?

Hand a strong person a sheet of paper and tell him that no matter how hard he tries, he won't be able to tear it.

6. A PENNY FOR YOUR THOUGHTS?

Place a penny on the floor and tell a subject its a very valuable penny, but that it's stuck to the floor, and no matter how hard he tries, he will not be able to lift it up.

Five Rules Of Suggestion

1. The first rule is to **ALWAYS ANTICIPATE**. If you see that a certain action or reaction is about to happen at any time now, or is happening, then suggest that is taking place. That way, in the subject's mind, YOU made it happen.

2. **REPETITION IS HYPNOTIC ITSELF**. By repeating suggestions, you keep the pace of the routine even. This is not a speed race. Give subjects time to absorb your ideas. Also, the monotony of your suggestions is hypnotic, helping the idea set in the mind.

3. **VOLUNTARY ACTIONS INCREASE SUGGESTIBILITY**. You can increase the chances of an involuntary action being accepted by employing voluntary actions, for example, having a person stand in a certain spot, place his hands a certain way, etc. Obedience to such commands tends to carry over to "bigger" suggestions.

4. **COMBINING SUGGESTIONS INCREASES INFLUENCE OVER OTHER SUGGESTIONS**. Suggestions used in combination reinforce the next one. The person stuck to the chair is a good example, building to hands glued to the head, to hands stuck to the seat.

5. **THE POWER TO PERSUADE IS ALL IN THE DELIVERY**. The proper delivery of a suggestion makes all the difference in the world. It's not just what you say, but *how* you say it. The tone, the inflection, your body movements, pauses, gestures, all have a suggestive influence on the subject.

Chapter

Other Sensational Stuff You Can Do

"In a minute I'm going to waken you...and when I do, you will continue to be able to hear my voice...but I will be invisible to you..."

Most hypnotic routines are actually post-hypnotic suggestions. Let's spent a few minutes exploring why subjects so readily accept and act out suggestions in hypnosis and when awakened.

Hypnosis is a state of mind in which ideas, or "suggestions" can easily be "sold" directly to the subconscious mind. We are bypassing the conscious mind. As explained earlier, *hypnosis is a way of getting directly into the subconscious mind, bypassing the critical evaluating facilities of the conscious mind, the source of our judgmental, evaluative, and critical abilities.*

Post-hypnotic phenomena, then, becomes an *expected occurrence.* Even though the person acting out the suggestion may be "awake" and in the active conscious state, the suggestion itself resides in the subconscious mind, triggered when told to. When the person acts out the suggestion, doing whatever it is you told him to, he is utterly powerless to overcome the effect of the suggestion. *His subconscious mind rules over his conscious state.*

We see it all the time in "real life." A person conditioned to smoking, one whose habit is so strong, so set in the subconscious mind, pulls a cigarette out, lights up, and begins puffing away, many times before he is even conscious of his actions. The suggestions you give under hypnosis works in the same way. You might tell the person they will bark like a dog whenever you say "pickles," the same as a smoker may be conditioned to smoke every time he finishes a meal, or feels under stress.

Let's examine two of the most interesting areas of post-hypnotic suggestion, *illusions* and *hallucinations*.

An *illusion* in hypnosis is the *false impression of an object.* This object then becomes the initial stimuli needed to form the illusion in the mind. For example, you might tell someone that an onion is actually a sweet, juicy apple. If the person is told to take a big bite, he will believe himself to be biting down on a sweet, juicy apple.

A *hallucination* is similar to an illusion, except *no material cue is needed*. To the subject, the object or sensation imagined is as real as real can be. For instance, you might tell someone that a bee is buzzing over his head, when nothing is really there. Hallucinations, then, are more powerful than illusions, because they *rely entirely on the strength of the suggestion alone,* with no visual cue to assist the mind.

The "Lemonade" Illusion

Here's an easy illusion to start off with, and it's a big crowd pleaser, too. Have a lemon sliced into four sections ready to hand the subject, and say, *"In a minute I'm going to awaken you, and since you've been such a good subject to work with, and knowing you must be a little thirsty by now, I've got something that will taste great and quench that thirst! A fresh, juicy, sweet Florida orange...Oh boy, this orange looks especially sweet. It should taste wonderful... SWEET AND JUICY...you're REALLY going to enjoy this orange...and after you wake, you will be unaware I have told you this, and of my telling you this now."* (There are any number of things you can use if you don't have a lemon. You can pass a raw potato off as an apple, or a glass of vinegar as a glass of homemade lemonade)

"...Okay, I'm about to wake you up, and let you enjoy this orange...Here we go... one...two... three...four, starting to wake...five... six...waking up more....seven...eight... waking... NINE...TEN...(snapping your finger) AWAKE!"

With the subject awake, *"Bill, you look pretty thirsty, Am I right?* (wait for a response)*...Why don't you take a bite of this sweet, juicy, delicious-tasting orange* (handing it to him)*...go ahead, it looks G-R-E-A-T, doesn't it?"* After he takes a bite or two, you should put a stop to it, saying, *"SLEEP!* (snapping your fingers)*... "*

Try this next, *"Bill, in a minute I'm going to wake you up again...and you'll still have your fresh, juicy, sweet Florida orange...SWEET AND JUICY...but, if you hear me say the word 'PIZZA,' you'll realize that what you have in your hand is actually a lemon...a sour, lip-puckering, tart lemon, and that you've been sucking on this LEMON!...but, unless and until I say the word 'PIZZA,' what you have in your hand is a sweet, juicy Florida orange...Do you understand, Bill? Good...and after you wake, you will be unaware I have told you this...and of my telling you this now."*

Water To Whiskey

Another variation on the above routine is to substitute water for whiskey, or whatever alcoholic drink you'd like. *"Bill, you look pretty thirsty, Am I right?* (wait for a response)*...How would you like a scotch on the rocks?....Go ahead, drink it right down...*(encouraging him to have two or three, he sinks into a state of believed intoxication, slurring his works and acting the part of the friendly drunk)*... "*

You get the idea from here.

The Invisible Man

Let's take a look at some routines involving hallucinations. This first one is a perfect example of how the mind can "see" whatever the mind can imagine. In this case, the mind will be convinced of what it *cannot* see.

With the subject asleep, *"In a minute I'm going to waken you...and when I do, you will continue to be able to hear my voice...but I will be invisible to you...I will remain in this room, but you will not be able to see me...no matter how hard you try...you will not see me...you can hear me...but you will NOT be able to SEE me...I will be invisible to you...completely invisible...you will see EVERYONE else in the room, and everything else will be completely normal, except you will not be able to see me, unless I tell you otherwise...Finally, after you wake, you will be unaware I have told you all of this, and of my telling you this now...*

"...I'm going to wake you now, and when I do, you will feel refreshed, renewed, full of energy...feeling wonderful about yourself and everything that's happened to you...Remember, I will be invisible to you...I will remain in this room, but you will not be able to see me...you can hear me...but you will not be able to see me...I will be invisible to you...completely invisible... unless I tell you otherwise...finally, after you wake, you will be unaware I have told you all of this, and of my telling you this now...Do you understand the instructions I've given you? If you do nod your head...(wait for response)...*very good...okay, here we go...one...two... three...four, starting to wake...five... six...waking up more....seven...eight...waking...NINE... TEN...*(snapping your finger) *AWAKE!"*

When the subject wakes, you should be standing off to the side of the person. *"Bill, how do you feel?"* Bill is looking around for you. *"Bill, I'm right over hear....*(as you say this, move to the other side of the subject)...*Bill, over here...*(moving again)....*over here..."*

By now, the subject is completely baffled. He hears you but he can't see a thing. You should next take a white handkerchief and tell the person you have brought your magic jumping hankie to entertain him. Starting at one end of the room, holding the handkerchief by two fingers, quickly bring it to the ground, then draw it up over your head, and as you proceed across the room, move it rapidly up and down, making the handkerchief appear to the subject to be flying. After all, he can't see you. To him, the hankie is propelled on its own power.

To finish off the routine say, *"Bill, when I snap my fingers, I will instantly be visible to you...*(snapping your fingers)."*

Bunny Love

Here's one more hallucination routine.

"In a minute I'm going to waken you,...and when I do, you will find that when you open your eyes, there will be a small, white furry rabbit in your hand...a cute, cuddly

baby rabbit...you will love this rabbit and have fun playing with it...get ready now...hold out your hand so you can look at the rabbit...

"*Remember, when I wake you, you will find that when you open your eyes, there will be a small, white furry rabbit in your hand...a cute, cuddly baby rabbit...you will love this rabbit and have fun playing with it...finally, after you wake, you will be unaware I have told you all of this, and of my telling you this now.....Okay, I'm about to wake you up,...here we go...one...two... three...four, starting to wake...five... six...waking up more... seven...eight... waking... NINE... TEN...(snapping your finger) AWAKE!*"

As the subject wakes up and looks at his hand, give him plenty of cues. "*Oh boy, is that a cute rabbit?...THAT is a cute rabbit...go ahead, pet the rabbit...he likes you...does he have a name? What's your rabbit's name?...*" As you get the subject involved, and as he is pantomiming playing with his imaginary rabbit, walk over and pretend to take the rabbit from his hands and set him on the floor.

"*Nice bunny...n-i-c-e bunny...OOPS...THERE HE GOES...your rabbit is getting away...YOU BETTER GO AND GET HIM!*" As the subject jumps from his seat to catch the rabbit, you should be giving him verbal suggestions..."*Oh, there he is over there! (pointing to one side of the room)...no, there he goes...OVER THERE!...*"

Pretending to catch the rabbit yourself, "hand it" to the subject, instructing him to take his seat again. For a big finish say, "*I don't know if I told you or not, but I can do magic with this rabbit, want to see?...You're probably familiar with the old magic trick of pulling a rabbit out of a hat...this is a variation on that theme...I'm going to make the rabbit disappear right out of your hands...watch carefully now...don't move your eyes away from your head...don't even blink...I'm about to make that bunny vanish...ready? one...two...three...GONE! The rabbit has disappeared! RIGHT BEFORE YOU EYES! (snapping your fingers)...SLEEP!...*"

Age Regression

The subconscious mind is an amazing thing. It stores memories of our entire lives! From the moment we are born, right up to the present. In the subconscious mind, memory can be told to be forgotten, too. You saw an example of that in the test where the subject is told he will forget his name.

Have you ever flashed back to an incident earlier in your life, maybe in a dream, that was so real, so vivid, it was almost like you were transported back in time, like you were actually there, watching as an outside observer, or a participant in the action? We're all capable of tapping into our hidden wealth of knowledge as we learn to penetrate our subconscious mind. Persons in a hypnotic state, deep in their subconscious have fantastic memories, with remarkable recall. You've probably heard of cases where the police have hypnotized a witness to a crime, only to have that person not only describe the perpetrator in great detail, but to give the authorities the license plate number of the getaway car!

One of the marvelous effects you can achieve with hypnosis is age regression, the ability to recollect childhood circumstances and situations with incredible accuracy and detail that would seemingly have been lost or forgotten years ago, lost, that is, to our ordinary memory. Yet, in the hypnotized state, they can easily be retrieved: what kind of clothes you wore to your third birthday; a Christmas present you received years earlier; a certain smell a room had when you were a child; a word-for-word conversation with a person long since dead.

There are a number of ways to conduct an age regression session. Here's one approach (for this example, we'll assume the subject is a 20-year old woman named Susan). With the subject asleep, *"Susan, I'm going to count to ten, and with each count, you will find yourself going back in time, drifting back a year or two at a time...ONE, I want you to think back to when you were younger...TWO, back to when you were a teenage girl in high school...drift back...b-a-c-k...THREE, to the tenth grade...to the ninth grade...FOUR, to the eighth... seventh... FIVE, back to when you were in elementary school...d-r-i-f-t-i-n-g further and further back in time...SIX, SEVEN...you're getting younger, and younger...smaller and smaller...EIGHT, back even further, to before you were in school...back...b-a-c-k...back before kindergarten...NINE, going back...drifting back in time...back...back...* (you can ask the subject where they are or how old they are)."

"...soon you will be four years old and it will be Christmas day...TEN, you're there...you're four years old and it's Christmas...you're in your house (or, you could pick a birthday party, first date, etc., or you can let the subject pick where she wants to stop -- *"You tell me when you've gone back to a time you want to stop at.").*"

Here are some questions you can ask to determine the best situation to explore: How old are you? Where are you? What are you doing? Who's in the room?)"...*Susan, how old are you?"* I'll detail some typical responses (In child's voice, giggling) S-e-v-e-n!"..."*Where are you?"*..."In my mommy and daddy's house"...*"What are you doing?"*..."Opening my presents!"...*"Who's in the room?"*..."Mommy and Daddy and Billy"...*"Who's Billy?"*..."My big brother!"

Usually one of two things will happen in age regression: subjects will lose complete awareness of their adult identity, regressing to a child-like behavior, reliving the experience as it happened; or see the experience as an adult, usually as an observer of the scene, removed from the actual events taking place.

In the example above, Susan has regressed back to childhood. Here's what the same thing would be like if Susan retained her adult identity. *"...picture yourself in your house...it's Christmas day 19__, you're ___ years old...Susan, how old are you?"* "I'm seven-and-a-half years old"...*"Where are you?"*..."In my mother and father's house, in the living room, by the Christmas tree"...*"What are you doing?"*..."I can see myself opening my Christmas presents!"... *"Who's in the room?"*..."My mother, father, and my brother Billy." If you have a subject who has regressed back in time, what's fun is to hand them a pad of paper and a pencil and ask them to write her name, or draw a picture.
Going back to a subject's school days can produce interesting results, too.

Ten More Sensational Routines

1. THE VIRGIN AND THE TRAMP

This routine requires one male and one female subject. The female subject is told she is a very experienced street hooker. The male is told he is a 15-year old virgin who is visiting the red light district for the first time. To the woman, *"When you wake, you are a very sexy, very experienced street hooker, on the prowl for tonight's lucky customer...business is a little bit slow tonight, so you'll need to really sell your services...by the way...you REALLY like your business, you're REALLY good at what you do...and you're not shy talking about it...Your 'street name' is Ginger..."*

To the man, *"When you wake, you are a 15-year old virgin, who is quite shy...but you're curious about sex, and want to speak with a street hooker who has some experience...but you don't know if you should 'save yourself' for the right woman..."*

2. ROCK-A-BY-BABY

In this routine, you tell one person she is a mommy, and the other a baby. The mother is suppose to take the baby in her lap and feed it a bottle, sing it a lullaby, and rock it to sleep.

To the woman, *"When you wake, you are a mommy with her baby* (say the other subject is a male) *boy...have your baby climb into your lap, feed it a warm bottle of milk, while you sing you baby a nice lullaby...like 'Rock-a-by-baby, on the tree top...' and rock the baby to sleep..."*

To the man, *"When you wake, you are a one-year old baby boy, and your mommy wants to fed you and rock you to sleep...which is one of your most favorite things to do..."*

3. MAGNETIC POWERS

In this routine, you will draw a person across the room. Having the subject standing at one end of the room, and you at the other, stretch out your hands, with your fingertips pointed at the subject, and say, *"As I draw in my hands like this* (bringing your hands in towards you, gesturing to come forward) *you will find yourself being pulled towards me...you will feel a powerful force draw you to me...as I do this* (gesturing with your hands)*, you will not be able to resist...you will move towards me...step by step...step by step...feel yourself drawn in by the force...closer...c-l-o-s-e-r..."*

A variation to this routine is to tell the subject that you have a lasso in your hand, which you pretend to whirl around your head. You tell the subject you are going to lasso him and pull him over to you. As you pretend to lasso him, act as though you have him roped, and then start to draw him towards you.

4. YOU CAN'T DO IT

With your finger, draw an imaginary line on the ground. Looking up at the subject, repeat, *"I've drawn a line on this floor...you will find that you can freely walk up to the line...but you will not be able to cross over it...the moment you try to cross...you will feel a force field blocking you...and the harder you try to cross the line...the more powerful the force field will become...if you try too hard, the force field will shove you backwards!"*

5. YOU'RE GETTING SLEEPY!

Place two subjects opposite each other, and tell them they are going to hypnotize each other. Then just stand back and watch the fun.

6. RUBBER NOSE

Tell a subject, *"When you wake you will find something different about yourself... you will discover that your nose and ears are made of rubber and can stretch...you can pull them out quite far, and when you let go...they'll snap right back....this will be a lot of fun...you'll love trying out your rubber nose and ears..."*

7. IS ANYTHING WRONG?

Pick a male and female subject. Taking the right hand of the female subject, place it on her right cheek and say, *"When you wake, you will be with your dream man...this person will be the guy you've been waiting for ALL YOUR LIFE...only one thing: your right hand will remain in the position it's in right now...you will not be able to remove your right hand...as hard as you may try...but you will try to pretend like nothing is wrong...you will ignore your right hand, and if your dream man asks you anything about your hand, you will find an excuse to tell him..."*

To the male subject, have him place make his right hand into a fist and place it under his chin, he too will not be able to remove his hand and will pretend everything is fine. The female subject, he will be told, is his dream woman.

To set the scene, tell them they just met on an train (or airplane, bus, laundromat, etc.), and that they are sitting next to each other. Have the man start the conversation off after they've been awakened.

8. A HOT DATE TONIGHT

Tell a male subject that *he* is a *she*, a beautiful female model, getting ready for a big date with a Hollywood producer.

"When you awake, you will be a beautiful FEMALE model...a gorgeous blond with an incredible body...tonight you have a big date with a Hollywood producer...he's looking for a new star for his movie...(bringing the subject over to a small table, complete with a mirror, lipstick, cosmetics, brushes and hair spray, etc.)... *you have just finished your shower and it's time to put your make-up on and do your hair...*When the subject is made-up, encourage him to look at himself in a hand mirror you give him. As he is admiring himself, wake him and tell him he is a man again. Boy, what a reaction you'll get!

9. SHOWER POWER

This is a great visual routine. Simple, but very effective. The subject is told that he just spent a day out in the hot sun, and it's time for a refreshing shower. You give him suggestions on adjusting the temperature, shampooing his hair, and then toweling off.

10. TENNIS ANYONE?

Tell your subject that he is at a tennis match. With you doing the color commentary, you describe a fictious match between Andre Agassi Boris Becker. You should be moving your head back and forth, in concert with where the ball is going. You can make this any kind of sports event: a baseball game, football, boxing, etc.

Chapter

Stage Hypnosis

"Like a circus show, where people sit on the edge of their chairs when the high-wire performers take to the skies of the big tent, or when the lion tamer enters the wire cage, the audience sits in awe waiting to see if you can "do the impossible," to witness the miracle of hypnosis."

Stage hypnotism has broad appeal. It's easy to see why. Stage hypnotism has everything. It's comedy, drama, mystery, and magic, all rolled into one. It's entertaining and educational. It's thought-provoking and engaging. It's capable of creating more thrills and chills than almost any other form of entertainment.

Stage hypnotism is unquestionably a daunting task for the performer, any performer! Unlike most stage acts, scripted to the word, every movement choreographed, then rehearsed and rehearsed until each show is a carbon copy of the last, most of stage hypnotism relies on the *human factor*. The actors and actresses in this play are spontaneous and real. No script for them. No rehearsals. Whatever happens, happens.

And you, as the hypnotist, must play three parts at once: the roles of lecturer, psychologist, and stage performer. The result is that each show is completely different. But, that's what makes this art form so fascinating and enjoyable to watch.

While depending on volunteers to make your show a success involves risk, there are a number of ways to minimize the possibilities of failure. And, in fact, there are a number of things you can do so that your show is almost guaranteed to be a huge hit.

The first rule to keep in mind is that you are there to entertain. So, while you have to be constantly concerned about inducing hypnosis and getting the subjects to respond to your commands, you must also be concerned about keeping the attention and interest of your audience. The best advice to give you is to be prepared. The more practice and experience you have as a hypnotist, the more it becomes second nature to you, and the more you can concentrate on the performance itself.

The showmanship side of stage hypnotism should be studied and practiced, too. If you're nervous or uncertain about what you're doing on stage, it will show. A whole group of people, your volunteers are going to constantly be looking at you for direction. If you waver at all, if you look like you are not in complete control of the situation, you could put the performance in jeopardy.

While what happens to the subjects is spontaneous, the show itself should be tightly scripted, at least your part, virtually word-for-word. You should know where the show is at all times, what routine is next, and how the pace of the show is going. Like any good stage performance, you need a opening, a middle, a climax, and a conclusion. And practice. Nothing is a substitute for the real thing. Practice your delivery and timing, your positioning on stage, and everything else that goes along with a good performance.

Stage hypnotism has a number of things working in its favor, not the least of which is the uncertainty involved. Like a circus show, where people sit on the edge of their chairs when the high-wire performers take to the skies of the big tent, or when the lion tamer enters the wire cage, the audience sits in awe waiting to see if you can "do the impossible," to witness the miracle of hypnosis.

Most people are rooting for you. There are always the disbelievers and skeptics, but you must play to those that are in your corner, capture that energy and uncertainty that hangs in the air, and turn it into part of the electrifying magic stage hypnotism offers.

And like the high-wire performer and the lion tamer, in the end, the audience wants to see you succeed. They want to believe. They want to be dazzled, to lean forward in their chairs captivated by your every word and action. They want to witness the show of the century, and you're going to give it to them.

The Opening Lecture

The opening lecture is one of the most critical elements in a successful stage performance. It sells the audience on you, and it wins over the willing subjects. Audience acceptance can make all the difference in the world. If you can win the audience over, they'll want to participate, to volunteer, to help the show to succeed. Conversely, if they do not feel like participating, the show will be lacking, or fail.

Since this portion of the show is all yours, and you control it one hundred percent, you should have your delivery down pat.

Before we go into the "patter," though, let's talk about who you'll be addressing, what kinds of audience types to expect. There is, of course, the non-believer, the skeptic, who assumes everything to be a sham. Next is the total believer, the person who willingly accepts what is about to happen, who ranges from the mildly convinced to the wildly enthusiastic. The last group, are the casual observers. They have no firm opinions, no prejudices. They come to be entertained, nothing more, nothing less.

The goal of the opening lecture is to appeal to all three groups. To quiet down the skeptic, to enliven the believers (and encourage volunteers from this group), and to arouse the interest of the casual observer to participate. By the time you finish your opening lecture, the entire audience should be saying, "I'm ready to be excited. I want to be entertained. Let's get going!"

With a stage set with little or no props except for a semi-circle of chairs, the number to correspond to the audience size, with a half-dozen to over a dozen chairs, you begin,

"Ladies and gentlemen, in just a few moments, I will invite a committee of people up on this stage to occupy these chairs (gesturing to the chairs) to take part in a number of scientific demonstrations in hypnotism. Before I do, though, and please, I ask that no one come up on the stage until asked to, let me describe for you what hypnosis is, and what will take place this evening...

"What is hypnotism?...Hypnotism, I should tell you, is the wonder science of the human mind...it is recognized and practiced by doctors and psychologists around the world. Oh sure, hypnotism was once greeted with skepticism. But, today it is openly acclaimed for its marvelous curative powers over the mind and body...

"Let me quickly dispel one misconception about hypnotism...that to be hypnotized, you must have a weak mind. That is utter nonsense. In fact, it has been proven scientifically that some of the very best hypnotic subjects are people of high intelligence. It takes a strong-minded, imaginative individual to focus his or her mind, to concentrate sufficiently, to achieve the best results...

"Hypnotism, according to most psychological studies, has been defined as an extension of concentration...in other words, it is the remarkable power that ideas possess when they claim our complete attention. Such dominant ideas are called suggestive ideas. Think of suggestion as the subconscious realization of an idea...let me repeat that: suggestion is the subconscious realization of an idea.

"I can best illustrate this by a little experiment in suggestion we can all try. Will you all join me? (waiting for the audience to respond)...Good!...Now here's what I'd like you to do...everyone sit back comfortably in your chairs, feet flat on the floor and rest your hands in your laps...Now direct your attention to me..."

Waking Suggestions: The Lemon Test

Your big, initial challenge with the audience will be to establish what is termed *suspension of disbelief.* We've all experienced it. Ever go to a movie or read a book, say, for instance, something with a science fiction theme, and your mind first says, *"But, this isn't real."* Yet, as you begin to get into the book or movie, as you begin to enjoy the experience, you *allow* yourself to believe that *it is real!* What's happening is that you are bypassing your critical facilities. This first experiment allows this suspension of disbelief to take place.

Holding a lemon in your hand and a knife in the other, *"Please observe this lemon I hold in my hand, and think about it this way: it is a yellow, bitter-tasting, acidy-bitter, sour juicy lemon...(as you cut into it and squeeze)...I will take this knife and cut into the lemon...and as I do, the bitter, sour juice drips on the floor. Now I'm going to suck that sour, bitter lemon juice* (sucking on the lemon, with gusto, with loud sucking noises, exaggeratingly puckering your lips)...*Boy, is this lemon bitter and tart! Whoa, that's sour!...And as I suck on this lemon, notice how your mouth begins to fill with saliva...*(keeping sucking on the lemon until you get enough of a response from the audience).

"There! See how you felt it...how you could almost feel the bitterness, the sour taste? That is the power of suggestion at work. The lemon provides you with an idea, an idea of something sour. That idea becomes realized unconsciously in your mind, the salivary glands secrete, and your mouth fills with saliva! That is the power of suggestion at work...that is the very force upon which hypnotism is based."

"You can also see why in a demonstration of this kind, in demonstrations of suggestion and hypnosis, the more you are able to concentrate upon the ideas presented, the more powerful will be the effects experienced...

Hand Magic

"Let's try another experiment...This time, I'd like you hold your hand out like this (palm facing towards the face, hand pointed up, and fingers held together) about a foot in front of your face, at nose level...pick a spot in the middle of the palm of your hand and focus all your attention there. As you concentrate, forget about anything or anyone else in the room...only listen to the sound of my voice...you may notice a couple of things. First, you may notice that your fingers will want to separate and open up. And secondly, you may notice that your hand will feel like it wants to move in towards your face. If either or both of these things begin to happen, let them. Don't force it to happen. But if it does, just allow it to happen...

"Right now, as you focus all your attention on that one spot, you may find it difficult to do. Shapes and colors may begin to emanate out from that spot, your eyes may begin to hurt. Keep focused. Only think of that one spot. As you do, imagine a force, an invisible force lightly pushing on the back of your hand, drawing it in towards your face...Concentrate on your hand being drawn in towards your face. You can feel the invisible force working, and as your hand moves in towards your face, the more it moves, the easier and faster it will happen."

There will be a number of people that will not respond at all to this experiment. For some, a mild sensation will occur. For others, the hand will move easily and the fingers completely separate. These people will be your best subjects, and you need to make note of who they are.

There is a strong psychological "game" that you need to play here. You must convince the audience that you are in command, that those people who succeeded in the two experiments did so because they most closely followed your instructions, and that those who were less successful did not.

One other thing you will notice, that will be critical to the success of your performance, is to feed subjects strong visual cues, ones that they can easily relate to. The lemon experiment is a good example.

So, when you want a subject to do something, say, move his hand in towards his face, give him a persuasive image to guide his actions and movements, like the idea of a "force" pushing on the hand.

Invitation On Stage

"Like I said before, in a few moments, I am going to request that any volunteers join me on stage. I ask only two things of all of those who do volunteer for these experiments in hypnotism tonight. The first is that you be sincere and serious about what we are doing. And, two, that you listen to everything I say, that you concentrate completely, and that you allow whatever happens to happen...

"I'm certain that whoever does volunteer will find the experiments to be very interesting...and I assure you now, that I will do my utmost to make this an enjoyable experience and one you will feel good about. With your cooperation, we can achieve some phenomenal results!

"So, without further ado, I invite all of those who would like to join me on stage to do so now (gesturing with your hands, waving them up on stage)*...to come forward and take any open seat...That's it, come on up!...".*

As people approach the stage, try to greet as many as possible, shaking their hands, welcoming them, all the while looking them squarely in the face. If more people come forward than you have chairs, have any additional people form a row standing directly behind the chairs.

As people are filling on stage, keep up the banter, *"That's right, step right up...there's plenty of room...take any seat...the more the merrier...come on up..."*

A couple of things to know. First, you are in charge. Exert your authority. Show the volunteers and the audience who's in control. Direct some people right to a specific chair, particularly those who exhibited good suggestive abilities in the previous tests. Have some people switch seats, even dismiss people you think are not sincere or may be disruptive. And don't seat couples together, or people that are from the same group. They tend to try and impress each other, and may talk in undertones, which can be very annoying. You should also try to alternate with male and female subjects. When you're satisfied with the arrangement, remark, *"Okay, that's much better. Now we're ready to begin!"*

So far, your purpose has been to establish a general positive tone for the attitude of the audience, and to encourage the most willing believers to step forward. Now, you need to lay down the rules, to lay the success or failure of the show deliberately in their laps.

"The ability to be hypnotized is a true skill. And as a skill, it naturally requires some talent in order to be accomplished. Now, some persons seem to inherently possess the ability, this talent to be hypnotized, while others have to develop it. It will be my objective this evening to help each and every one of you to enter this remarkable state of mind called hypnosis."

What you've done in the last minute or so is to strictly lay the success or failure of the show in the volunteers' laps, and now, to tell them that being hypnotized is a skill, and in so doing, putting up the challenge of *"Do you have what it takes?"*

For the skeptic, he is now in a tough spot. If he doesn't go along with you, in the eyes of the audience, he admits his inadequacy. For the believer, it just helps to reinforce his feelings. For the skeptic and the believer alike, there is tremendous peer pressure that goes with being part of the stage group, making it difficult to buck the tide. What choices they have quickly narrow: get along, or get out!

This is the old "double bind." They have to follow along, or risk looking dumb. It's no longer a matter of you against them, of challenging your powers of hypnosis against their powers to resist. Everyone should be pulling in the same direction, everyone has the same objective: to be hypnotized.

With everyone seated, with the audience ready to be entertained, and volunteers all in position, you can begin the next facet of the show, the preparation for induction.

"Everyone, please give me your complete attention. We have more volunteers than we need and that this stage will comfortably accommodate, and so I am going to give you a test, and those that are able to concentrate the best will continue on, and others will be asked to return to their seats...If I do ask you to be seated, please take no offense, it merely means that I believe you will enjoy the show more from your seat in the audience...You see, some people are able to concentrate and enter hypnosis easier than others. Some are very quick, while others take more time. Let's try this experiment together, and then we can tell..."

Eyes Open Test

"It's another good example of the power of suggestion...What I'd like everyone to do is relax in your seat, place your feet firmly on the ground, and rest your hands in your lap. Now close your eyes...Close them together very tightly...tight...very tight...Now, with your eye lids closed, I want you to roll your eyes up, up to the top of your head...imagine yourself trying to look up through the top of your head...Squeeze your eye lids together tighter...they are becoming stuck...stuck so tight...completely stuck...that's it...keep looking up, looking back to the top of your head...feel your eye lids stuck tightly together...they cannot open...no matter how hard you try, your eye lids will not open...try...try hard!...Hard!...See, they won't open."

You want to be closely observing the volunteers at this point. Many people will be struggling to open their eyes. Many will not be able to do it. After a few seconds, say, *"All right. You can open your eyes now! Relax...open your eyes!"*

This is a good test because, as explained previously, the small muscles around the eyes are very susceptible to suggestive influence, combined with the physiological fact that it is impossible to open your eye lids with the eyes rolled back in your head.

At this point, you want to begin eliminating some of the subjects. Anyone who opened their eyes or had a big grin on their face should be dismissed. Walk directly over to these people, tap them on the shoulder and quietly ask them to leave the stage and return to their original seats. Have them leave as quietly as possible, so as not to disturb the others.

Now you've removed many of the unwanted persons from the group, leaving the best of the subjects. Psychologically, this also acts as positive reinforcement for the remaining group.

The Arm Stretch Test

With the reduced group, continue with, *"You've just witnessed once again the power of suggestion. That the more you concentrate the greater the effects achieved...Let's try one more simple test...This time I'd like everyone to fastening their hands together, interlocking your fingers, and raise your arms above your head, locking your elbows...now turn your hands up, so that your palms face up...lock your fingers tightly...squeeze tightly...tight...*

"Stretch your arms straight...squeeze your fingers...very tightly...keep your attention on me...concentrate on what I say...your arms are becoming stiff and tense...your hands are becoming locked together...stuck tight...stuck together...squeezing tightly...squeezing your finger together tightly...locked in place...your fingers are stuck so tightly that they will not come apart...no matter how hard you try...see, you cannot pull them apart...try and pull them apart...you cannot! They are stuck..."

Again, you want to eliminate anyone able to pull his hands apart. To the others you say, *"Please step forward forming a line in front of me, and as I touch your hands, I will release them...they will instantly separate!"*

Now you have your hypnotic group. Ask them to take the seat you assign, directing each person to a specific chair. Now you have the best subjects, they've been pre-conditioned, and we're ready to begin the main part of the show.

The Main Performance

To the subjects on stage, say, *"Let me take this opportunity to thank all of our wonderful volunteers. I will do my best to make your visit on stage most interesting..."*

Turning to the audience, *"And to all of you in the audience, I hope you will forgive me for turning my back to you from time to time as I address our volunteers. And please, at the beginning of these experiments, I must ask that you refrain from laughing, as it disturbs the people here on stage in their efforts to completely concentrate...As we go along in the show, and I will let you know when, you may laugh as freely as you wish...but, for now, please sit back in silence and observe the events that are about to take place..."*

Turning back towards the subjects, *"Let's have everyone give their name and where they are from, starting from my left and working to the right..."* Try to pick up on the names, remembering as many as you can.

"I'd like to start things off with an experiment in relaxation. First, I will ask that each of you sit back comfortably in your chairs, placing your feet flat on the floor, and resting your hands in your lap, placing each hand on each of your knees ...very good!...

"Now if you would all direct your complete attention towards me, and pay particularly close attention to everything I say to you, every suggestion given, and every idea I put forth..."

"The ability to be hypnotized is a skill that each of you can develop with practice, and it is the objective this evening, on this stage, to practice together to develop this skill..."

Be sure that you try to divide your attention evenly among the subjects, making everyone feel they have your undivided attention.

"To be hypnotized, you must be able to relax, while at the same time concentrating continuously...and as I give you these thoughts to think about, concentrate like this: For example, if I should say that your arms are becoming heavy and that your arms are pressing down in your lap, think to yourself that your arms are becoming heavy and that your arms are pressing down in your lap...and as you do, you will find that your arms are, indeed, feeling heavier, just as I suggested..."

"All right, then, everyone think first of relaxing your head, or relaxing the muscles of the top of your head...and as you do, feel a tingling sensation happening in your scalp...and as you concentrate more on your head, relaxing the muscles, you will feel the gentle tingling feeling...now let that thought move down your face...into your neck...feel your neck relaxing...feel your neck muscles relax...into the muscles in your shoulders...relaxing more...down through your chest...across your back...down your thighs...feel yourself sinking into the chair...feeling your body getting heavy...sinking deeper into the chair...feel it in your legs...down to your feet...feel your legs getting heavy...sinking down...feet firmly planted on the floor...feet and hands very heavy..."

You should be positioned in the middle of the volunteers, staring out at them, focusing your stare through them, looking at them at a spot just above their eyes, and on a point two feet behind them.

"It feels so good, feel your muscles relax...feel your body relax...it feels good to relax...and as you relax, you can feel your eye muscles relax...your eyes feeling heavy...burning a little from being so tired...tired and heavy...your eyelids are growing heavier and heavier...you are getting sleepier and sleepier...eyes wanting to close...eyes v-e-r-y h-e-a-v-y, they want to close...I will count to three, and on the count of three, everyone close your eyes...ready...ONE...eyes heavy...TWO...eyes closing...THREE...EYES CLOSED!"

The Deepening Phase

"That's right...relax...forget about your eyes...just allow yourself to drift off...drift off into sleep...s-l-e-e-p...d-e-e-p s-l-e-e-p...drifting deeper and deeper...deeper and deeper and deeper...very deep!...Feel your head moving down to your chest...feel your whole body grow very relaxed and loose...(placing your hand on the back of any subject who isn't responding directly to this command, slowly ease them down in the chair)...with every breath you take, with every beat of your heart...you will find yourself going deeper and deeper to sleep...drifting deeper and deeper, deeper and d-e-e-p-e r.*

"I want you to picture yourself at the top of a staircase. It's a wide staircase with a railing you can hold on to if you want. These are very nice stairs. You will notice that there are ten steps leading down to the landing below. We are going to slowly take a walk down these stairs, and as we do, you will notice that with every step you take, you will become more and more relaxed...that with each step, you will fall deeper and deeper into this state of relaxation that you're in now...We're taking that first step...becoming more relaxed...second step...going deeper and deeper to sleep...the third step, still deeper...the fourth step...getting very, very relaxed...the fifth step, we're half way down the steps....going down deeper and deeper, feeling better and better...the sixth step...the seventh step...DEEP...DEEPER...VERY DEEP SLEEP...the eight step, almost at the bottom, deeper still...the ninth step...ten step...TOTALLY relaxed...deep, deep sleep...

"Now I want you to pay close attention to every suggestion that I give you. As you sit in your chair, calm and rested, you are aware of everything going on around you and every word I say...In fact, your mental processes are becoming intensified, become sharpened...so that you will find you can concentrate easily and powerfully upon every suggestion that I give you...You will find that you can follow and accomplish each demonstration you try...calm and rested, you can concentrate easily and powerfully upon every suggestion that I give you...nothing will disturb you...you will follow and accomplish each one perfectly...

"In a few moments, I'm going to wake you, and when I do, you will feel refreshed, renewed, full of energy...feeling wonderful about yourself and everything that's happened to you...To do this, to waken you, I will count to ten, and by the time I reach 'ten' and say the word 'AWAKE!,' you will be wide wake. Again, I will count to ten, say 'AWAKE,' and you will be wide awake, you will immediately open your eyes, you will sit up in your chair, feeling exactly the same as you do when you wake up in the morning after a good night's sleep....And, anytime I want you to go back to this sleep, to the state of relaxation you're in now, all I will do is SNAP MY FINGERS and say the word 'SLEEP!' and you will INSTANTLY CLOSE YOU EYES and drift off into this sleep...In fact, when I say the word 'SLEEP,' you will drift off into a sleep much, much deeper than the one you're in now, you will fade into a d-e-e-p, d-e-e-p, D-E-E-P S-L-E-E-P ...Do you understand the instructions I've given you? If you do nod your head...(wait for response)*...very good. Again, I'll count to ten, and then say the word 'awake!,' and you will open your eyes and be wide awake, remembering everything that's taken place so far today...and anytime I say the word 'SLEEP,' and snap my finger you will IMMEDIATELY close your eyes and drift off into a sleep even deeper than the one you're in now...Ready? Nod if you are...*(look for response)*...okay, here we go...one you're sleeping deeply, but now it's time to get up...two... beginning to wake up...three...four...feeling very good...five...six...waken up more...seven...eight...waking...NINE...TEN...*(snapping your finger) *AWAKE!"*

If you want to speed up the process of putting subjects back to sleep, you might want to give them a visual cue only to sleep, rather than a voice and visual cue (snapping fingers, saying *"SLEEP!"*). For instance, you might tell them, *"The moment I look at you and point my finger at you, you will instantly go to sleep."*

At this point, you have the subjects under your control, and the audience convinced they're in for quite a show. Nothing spectacular has occurred, yet, but the electricity is starting to charge the air!

Right now, most of your volunteers are in a mild hypnotic state. Some may be deeper, others may not have responded well. If you have anyone who is not in the hypnotic trance by now, quietly dismiss them, excusing it as wanting to make the group a little more intimate. And, of the remaining people, you should have a fairly good idea who your best subjects are, who are the most responsive members of the group. After some practice, you'll be able to quickly spot your top subjects.

Walking over to one of these people, start a dialogue. Be sure to position yourself off to the side to not block the view of the audience. Don't upstage your subjects. You may want to crouch down on your knees if that helps. Taking the subject's right hand in your right hand, shake hands, but don't let go. Hold on lightly to the person's hand (it should be loose and limp). *"Hello there...how are you...*(waiting for a verbal response)...*and your name is....*(let's say its a female subject named Jane)...*Jane, That's a lovely name, Jane... Jane...*(snapping your fingers and pulling her down with the right hand) *SLEEP!...* and as you say this, place your left hand on the side of the subject's head and help lower her head into her lap, with her hands extended outward...

"Jane, drifting deeper and deeper...d-e-e-p-e-r and d-e-e-p-e-r...listening to every word I say...allowing yourself to fall deeper and deeper to sleep...deeper and deeper...Jane, I want you to think about your right hand...as I reach over and touch your wrist, I want you to imagine that I am attaching a giant helium balloon on a string to your wrist...the string is tied around your wrist...feel the string gently pulling on your wrist (watching for responses)... *there, it's tugging on your wrist, lightly, up...up...up...feel the balloon lifting your hand into the air...your hand is very light...lifting up and up...u-p and u-p...now TWO balloons are tied to your wrist...two GIANT helium-filled balloons... pulling on your wrist...lifting your hand...and as they rise higher and higher in the air, the balloons are getting bigger and bigger, and as they do, your hand is feeling lighter and lighter...now there are three balloons...four balloons... five...six...SEVEN....EIGHT...NINE...T-E-N GIANT HELIUM-FILLED BALLOONS...your hand is very, very light...lifting up and up...pretty soon the balloons will start to almost l-i-f-t you out of your chair...higher and higher...higher and higher..."*

Turning to another subject, and we'll assume there are five volunteers left (although you can easily accommodate a dozen people or more on stage at one time), position yourself next to this subject and taking his hand as before (just leave Jane alone...you may want to occasionally say, *"Jane...feel the helium balloons lifting you higher and higher...higher and higher..."*), *"Hi. Larry, isn't it?* "Yes..." *"Larry,* (snapping your fingers) *SLEEP!"* Quickly take your hand and lowering his head to his lap. This time, you want to make it even more dramatic than with Jane. This subject has hardly spoken one word, and he is out cold.

"Larry, I want you to relax completely...just allow yourself to drift off...drift off into sleep...s-l-e-e-p...d-e-e-p s-l-e-e-p...drifting deeper and deeper...deeper and deeper and deeper...very deep!...Your whole body is growing limp and loose...limp and loose...your muscles are very loose...drifting deeper and deeper to sleep...(taking both of your hands, gently help the subject to slide out of his chair and onto the floor)...*totally relax, Larry...drift off into a deep, deep sleep...d-e-e-p, d-e-e-p sleep..."*

Now you should get up and go to another person, a male. Positioning yourself to the side of this person, address him this way, *"Hello there! How are you?* (wait for response)...*How do you like the show so far?"* (wait for response -- remember, he's seen two people go under your spell as some as they gave their name, conditioning him to do the same)...*"Larry looks like he's enjoying himself, doesn't he?..."* (holding your hand out that you used with the last two people, slowly bring it up next to the subject's head, but out a foot or two, saying, *"And what's your name, may I ask?"* "B-B-Bill..." *"Bill, S-L-E-E-P!"* And, in slow motion, move your hand across, not touching, but close enough to Bill's face that he begins to move off to the side, not downward, but to the side, and help him along by easing his body down, so that his head is resting in on the lap of the female subject next to him. Let's call her Debbie.

Next, turn your attention to the subject seated on the end, say it's Cathy. *"Well hello there. How are you? ....Good! Looks like Bill is a l-i-t-t-l-e b-i-t sleepy, wouldn't you say?"* Turning to Debbie, *"You don't mind Bill taking a nap in your lap, do you...good, I'm sure Bill doesn't mind, either..."*

Back to Cathy, *"Cathy, you know what I'm about to do?"* Knowing she's about to be put to sleep, only hightens the anticipation of the event, making it even more pronounced. *"Cathy...yes, I want you to (snapping your fingers) SLEEP! Deep, deep sleep, put your head back Cathy...rest it against the back of the chair...that's it...deep sleep, drifting deeper and deeper...with every breath you take...with every beat of your heart...sinking deeper and deeper to sleep...Cathy, I want you now to think of the funniest joke you know, and when you get to the punch line, you're going to find it very funny, funnier than ever before, so funny you will start laughing out loud, and you will find the laughter contagious...it will make you laugh even more...and you will laugh at yourself laughing...because your laughter is funny..."*

Turn to the two remaining subjects, we'll name them Mark and Debbie, *"Mark, I want you to please stand and walk towards me. Now stand very still and straight, hands by your side... whatever happens, you will remain standing unless I tell you otherwise...Do you understand?...Mark, I want you to look me squarely in the eye...I want you to SLEEP!... Deep...deep sleep...drifting off into a deep sleep...Mark, I'm going to position myself in back of you. I will be standing right in back. In a moment you will find your entire body start to stiffen up...your arms will stiffen, your back will stiffen, your legs will stiffen...your body will become rigid...as hard and rigid as a board...HARD, RIGID...AS STIFF AND HARD AS A STEEL ROD..* (As you do this, lightly squeeze the person's shoulders to emphasize the point. It also allows you to check for rigidity)... *HARD...STIFF...RIGID...so hard and rigid, that if I hold on to your shoulders and gently place you on the floor, your body will not bend or move at all...* (placing his rigid body on the floor)."

"Oooh Debbie...Debbie...it's your t-u-r-n...are you ready?...I think you are!...Here we go.... (to add drama, be standing 10 or 15 feet from the subject, and slowly move your whole body and your arms down in the direction of the Bill ...indicating with your hand, gesturing that you want her to lie down on top of Bill, who is lying in her lap) She has just seen all of her peers follow you, she will find it impossible to resist.

I've just shown you how to hypnotize six subjects. You can hypnotize 16 or 60 the same way.

We now have the audience sitting on the edge of their chairs, and the subjects obeying your every command. The show is moving now. At this point, you need to increase the tempo and liven up the routines.

An Alternate: Instant Hypnosis

If you want to add some real drama to your show, just after you have everyone close their eyes, before the deepening session, try this. Turn to the audience, and say, *"We've talked a lot tonight about hypnosis...and I've promised you a scientific demonstration...what you are about the witness will defy logic...it will happen so fast...I caution you not to turn away or to talk...you may miss it, it will happen that fast...What I'm about to do is to instantly hypnotize one of the people on this stage..."*

Pick one of your best volunteers. Let's say it's one of the female subjects. Go over to the person, making very close eye contact, and maintaining the eye-to-eye contact, take her right arm in your right hand, holding it, repeat, *"Hello...how are you?...(the subject responds)...very good. Thank you for being a part of the show. Your name was Jane, I believe. Is that right?* (while you're doing this, slowly shaking her hand, softly enough that its not too obvious, but enough that you can tell if she is relaxed.). As she begins to answer, Look her in the eye, and pull down gently on her arm as you say, *"SLEEP!* (snapping your fingers), taking your left hand and applying downward pressure to the subjects right shoulder, and using your right arm, quickly bring her down, head in her lap. Then say, *"Jane, drifting deeper and deeper...d-e-e-p-e-r and d-e-e-p-e-r. to sleep...listening to every word I say...allowing yourself to fall deeper and deeper to sleep...deeper and deeper...*

Standing up, move across the stage walking past all of the subjects. When you get to the end, slowly spin around, turning to one of the subjects nearest you, catching his attention, eyeball-to-eyeball, point your finger directly at his head, and shout, *"SLEEP!"* as he instantly drops off. In quick succession, you now proceed along the row, hypnotizing the other people.

The Routine

Before we jump into the routines that will make up the body of the show, let's review what's happened so far. You've sold the audience on your abilities, and, as a result, a group of volunteers willingly agrees to take part in the stage performance. You identified the best of those people, they were hypnotized, and have gone through the deepening process.

A couple of things are very important to keep in mind, here. The first is that you must train your audience to respond the way you want them to: to have them "pump up" the subjects. To do this, you need to give them encouragement, saying, for example, *"Hey, these folks on stage are doing a wonderful job, don't you think? Let's give them a big round of applause to show our appreciation. What do you say?"*

This spurs on the subjects to want to please you and the audience, and to feel a part of the success the show is having. This psychology, subjects pleasing the audience and feeling the pride of being one of the performers, is one of the things that makes hypnotic effects in stage hypnotism much more pronounced and dramatic than in a one-on-one session. Use it to your advantage.

And don't let your subjects feel that they are the butt of the joke, to be made fun of. Rather, that they are the center of attention and that they want to elicit the laughter and applause of the audience. Let them know this by saying, *"Everything we're going to do tonight is for FUN. Everyone here wants to enjoy themselves. Whatever you do, whatever happens is all in fun. The entire evening is all for FUN. You, right along with everyone else, will have a wonderful time and have plenty of fun."*

Also, remember that having completed one series of suggestions, always remove them before presenting any new set of suggestions, or one might conflict with the other. *"Jane, Larry, Bill, Cathy, Mark and Debbie, when I clap my hands, the effects you are experiencing will be completely gone...you will resume your relaxed state..."*

Okay, we're ready to continue the show. The tempo is building. Let's not only pick up the pace, though, let's start to get some interaction going between the subjects.

The Domino Effect

Approaching one of the subjects, say, *"When you wake, and until I tell you otherwise, you will not be able to remember your own name. You have completely forgotten your name. But, if you hear the name 'FIDO', I want you to bark like a dog. Every time you hear me say 'Fido" you will bark, one time each time you hear me say it and the more you hear it, the louder you will bark..."*

To the next person say, *"When you wake, and until I tell you otherwise, every time you hear the sound of a dog barking, you will MEOW once like a kitten, and the more you hear barking, the louder you will meow..."*

To the next subject, *"When you wake, and until I tell you otherwise, every time you hear the sound of a kitten meowing, I want you to sing 'God bless America, land that I love'...sing it loud and clear..., like this* (demonstrate)..."

To the next volunteer say, *"Every time you hear someone sing 'God Bless America,' I want you to quietly wait, standing at attention, and put your hand across your heart...and when the song is over, yell out, 'PLAY BALL,' and then sit down..."*

To the last person (this should be a woman), say, *"Every time you hear the words, 'Play ball,' I want you to look over at that person and say, 'Turn off that stupid TV and come to dinner...NOW!"*

Okay, now we've set up a sort of comic chain reaction. One person will set off the next, and on down the line. All we need to do is light the fuse! After waking everyone, turn to the first person and say, *"Excuse me, I seem to have forgotten your name. What did you say your name was?"* Unable to think of it, and looking perplexed, you add, *"Was it Willy? No...that's not it...Was it Billy? No that's not it...Was it Fi...Fi...Fi...FRED?...No, that's not it...How about F-I-D-O?"*

Bingo! The magic word. He barks, the next person meows, the next sings the national anthem, another shouts "play ball," and the last yells out to come to dinner. To keep it going, all you need to do is say the magic word again.

The More The Merrier

The More the Merrier is similar to the *Domino Effect*. It relies on the same principle of suggestions that play off each other in rapid succession. Here's a bit for three people.

In this routine, the first person is told, *"When you awaken, everything will be fine, but if I clap my hands, you will have an uncontrollable urge to run over to that tape recorder* (pointing to a table on stage with a tape player -- or it could be a record player or CD player), *and turn it on and then run back to your seat and sit down again..."*

To the second subject say, *"When you wake, everything will be fine, but if someone starts to play the tape (record, CD) player you will jump out of your seat and move to the front center of the stage and start to sing the words of the song as loud as you can..."*

To the last subject, *"When you wake, everything will be fine, but if someone starts to play the tape (record, CD) player, as soon as that person sits back down, and make sure you wait until they're seated, I want you to rush over to the player and turn it off, then sit back down..."*

Awakening everyone, you can start into a discussion about music. Looking at the audience, say, *"I've brought some music with me today, and since we're about mid-way in the show, I thought you'd like to hear a tune. If you like the music, show me by clapping your hands like this...* (clap your hands)."

Once again, the chain-reaction starts. Subject one rushes to turn on the music, subject two moves center stage, and as subject one takes a seat, subject three races to turn off the music...as he does, you clap your hands...off they go again. Because you control the timing of the routine by your clapping, you can easily speed up or slow down the pace, as you see fit.

X-Ray Vision

This is a variation of the *X-Ray Eye* routine discussed in Chapter 6, *except in mass*. Note the difference in how this routine is presented on stage, with several volunteers, versus a smaller, more intimate setting. Clearly, many of the routines discussed in earlier chapters, with few changes, can be adapted to the stage.

The routine starts out something like this: *"In a minute I'm going to waken all of you, before I do, though, I want to give you something...it's my own invention...I call it my 'X-RAY EYE'...it can do amazing things, as you're about to discover* (handing the X-Ray Eyes to each subject)...*Now let me tell you something about the object you hold in your hand....I call it my X-Ray Eye because, when you look through the hole in the middle of it, you can see through clothing...that's right, you can see right through peoples' clothing...and, you know what else is great? No one will know you can see them naked....ISN'T THAT GREAT?*

"...Don't do anything with your X-Ray Eye yet...let me tell you more...Like I said, when you look through the eye, you will be able to see people naked...they won't know you can see them naked...that will be fun...Now, there are two other things you need to know...The first is that I'm wearing special protective clothing and you won't be able to see ME naked...The second is that if I catch you looking through the X-Ray Eye, I'm going to have to take it away from you...So if you see me looking at you, HIDE THE X-RAY EYE...Again, you will be able to see everyone but me naked...and if I catch you looking at anyone, I have to take your X-Ray Eye away...Make sure you keep it hidden...You might want to put the hand you have it in now behind your back, so no one can see it...

"...Okay, I'm about to wake you all up...once more, you can't let me catch you using the X-Ray Eye, so hide it in your hand or somewhere else whenever I look your way...otherwise, you're free to stare at anyone you want...finally, after you wake, you will be unaware I have told you all of this, and of my telling you this now...

"...Here we go...one...two... three...four, starting to wake...five... six...waking up more...seven...eight...waking...NINE... TEN...(snapping your finger) *AWAKE!"*

With the subjects awake, turn towards the audience and start a dialogue. While you do this, the subjects have probably taken out the *Eye* and are staring intently at each other and the audience.

Give the volunteers five to ten seconds, before announcing, *"HEY, WHAT'S GOING ON?"* (to give them time to hide the Eye again) then whirl around and say, *"Is there something going on around here I'm not aware of?"* You'll normally get a set of sheepish responses.

On some other pretext, turn your back to the subjects once more. You can expect all the stage members will whip out their *Eyes* again. The noise and laughter of the crowd will tip you off. When it happens, go through the same bit again, allowing them time to palm the *Eye*, and pretending to miss what's going on.

Once more, fake an excuse, turning your back. When the action starts, say, *"You people better not be using one of those X-Ray Eyes that I've heard about. If you are, I'll have to take it away from you!"*

You can continue this indefinitely, but when you're ready to move on to the next routine, remember to remove the suggestion. Back in the sleep state, repeat, *"Your magic X-Ray Eye has lost its ability. You can no longer look through clothing with it. It's now just a piece of cardboard with a hole in the middle."*

Saturday Matinee

This routine can involve all of your stage volunteers. Tell them that when they awaken they will be at a movie theater, watching a wonderful film. *"In a few moments, I'm going to wake you, and when I do, you will see a giant motion picture screen in front of you, and on the screen will be a comedy...a very funny film...it's so funny, you'll find it difficult not to laugh...*

"I will count to ten, say 'AWAKE,' and you will be wide awake, you will immediately open your eyes, you will sit up in your chair, feeling exactly the same as you do when you wake up in the morning after a good night's sleep....And, anytime I want you to go back to this sleep, to the state of relaxation you're in now, all I will do is SNAP MY FINGERS and say the word 'SLEEP!', and you will INSTANTLY CLOSE YOU EYES, and drift off into this sleep...In fact, when I say the word 'SLEEP,' you will drift off into a sleep much, much deeper than the one you're in now. You will fade into a d-e-e-p, d-e-e-p, D-E-E-P S-L-E-E-P...

"Again, when I wake you, you'll see a movie screen in front of you and be able to see and hear the movie...and after you wake, you will be unaware I have told you this, and of my telling you this now...

"Okay, get ready to watch the movie!...here we go...one you're sleeping deeply, but now it's time to get up...two... beginning to wake up...three... four...feeling very good...five... six...waken up more...seven...eight... waking... NINE...TEN...AWAKE!.

The subjects should all be awake, sitting up straight in their chairs and staring straight ahead, facing the audience and the imaginary screen, as you guide them along, *"Oh boy, this is a real funny picture...that guy is hysterical...he is really funny...I MEAN FUN-NY!...I've never seen anyone so funny, have you?...if you want to laugh out loud, go right ahead...(you start laughing)...Ha!...Ha!...Ha!..."*

Once you get everyone in the laughing mood and the whole stage is in hysterics, say, *"Oh my...this is not funny any more...the story is very serious...that MEAN MAN is evicting that POOR woman and her CHILDREN...he's throwing them out of their home...those children look so sad...the mother has nothing...no money...no food...only torn rags for clothes...this is the SADDEST THING I'VE VERY SEEN...now it's beginning to snow...it's freezing outside...the children don't have winter coats...I...I feel like crying...I'm sorry....this is too much...(acting like you're crying).."*

As the subjects start to respond, and some may cry, you want to change the mood again, saying, *"OH!...LOOK AT THAT, the woman is saved by the rich King who marries her, and they all move to his castle...oh, oh, it's getting funny again...there's that comic...he is so funny...ha...ha...ha!...I can't help myself...isn't he the funniest guy you've ever seen?...go ahead...laugh....laugh out loud...it's perfectly all right...(switching again)...*

"Boy oh boy, look at what's happening now...the chase scene...those cars are going really fast...zoom, left turn! (leaning your body heavily to the side as you say it)...zoom! hard right turn!...LOOK OUT...LOOK OUT...THAT BRIDGE IS A DRAW BRIDGE AND IT'S GOING UP...HE'LL NEVER MAKE IT...OH NO!...STOP...STOP...HE CAN'T STOP...HE'S GOING UP THE RAMP........HE MADE IT! Boy, was that a close one!...Now the picture is fading from the screen...fading...fading...it's all gone...(snapping your finger)...SLEEP!"

Fountain of Youth

This is a great visual routine that will impress any audience. For this, you'll need two subjects. Let's say it's Larry and Bill.

"Larry and Bill, I'd like you to join me in a scientific experiment...I have in my hands two very remarkable bottles. In one is special water (holding up one bottle) *from the original Fountain of Youth. Drink from it, and you immediately regress back in age, going back in time, returning to your youth...in the other* (hold up the other bottle) *is water from Methuselah's tomb. Drinking it will cause you to grow into an old man in seconds..."*

Turning to one of the subjects, *"Larry, I offer you the Elixir of Youth. Drink from it and grow young!"* As he starts drinking it, stare at the two bottles (with one in each hand), quickly looking at one, then the other, back and forth, turning your head to the left, then right, then back. Looking confused, say, *"Oh my...oh my, Larry, I made a BIG mistake! I gave you the waters of Methuselah...you will start to grow old...you will begin to feel yourself growing older...being catapulted past your present age...you are becoming older...and older...and older...the waters are turning you into an old man...you're 40...50...60...70...80 years old!...Larry, you're an old man!"*

As you are saying this, the subject should be responding in kind. He should be showing visible signs of aging.

"Larry, here, let me get you a chair to sit in., and here's a cane to hold on to. You look very old and tired. Please don't strain yourself. Have a seat. Larry...I don't know what to say...I apologize for the mix-up...I'll straighten it out in a second...I still have the waters from the Fountain of Youth...we'll have you young again...you'll see."

Turning to Bill, *"Bill, we gave Larry the wrong bottle...but, now we know which is which...*(holding up and pointing to the other bottle)*...THIS is the elixir that will make Larry young again...I want you to show the audience and Larry how drinking this will make you young...*(handing him the bottle)*...drink Bill drink!..."* As he drinks, *"Bill, the waters are already beginning to take effect...you are getting younger and younger...you are a teenager...now you're ten...nine...eight...seven...six...five...four...three... two...one years' old.... Bill, you're a baby, you're back to crawling on the floor...Bill, you're...you're...becoming younger still...you're going back so far, you're in your mother's womb...Bill, you're in your mommy's tummy..."*

Returning to Larry, *"Larry, we'll have you fixed up in a second...here, drink some of this...the waters from the Fountain of Youth...you will regain your same age as when we started our experiment..."*

As he drinks from the bottle, quickly hand the other bottle to Bill, saying *"Bill, here is the bottle with Methuselah's water...drink it and you will regain your age...See! You're getting older...you're a baby...you're one...two...growing older..."*

Very quickly turning to Larry, *"Larry, I can see you regaining your youth...you're getting younger...and younger...and younger...seventy...sixty... fifty...forty...now you've returned back to the original age you were when we started....wait, what's this! Larry, you're going back past your present age, you're twenty...ten...nine...eight..."*

Spinning back to Bill, *"Bill, what's happening...you're ten...twenty...thirty... forty...fifty...sixty...seventy...eighty! Eighty years old. We gave you too much of Methuselah's water. Bill, here, take Larry's cane..."*

Turning to Larry, *"Larry! Oh my, Larry, you're growing younger...and younger...now you're four...three...two...one...a baby...you're...you're...becoming younger still...you're going back so far, you're in your mother's womb...Bill, you're in your mommy's stomach..."*

Now we've not only had both subjects change age, one to grow old, the other to regain his youth, we've completely reversed the process. Now for the finish.

To the audience, "Ladies *and gentlemen...I'm afraid our experiment has gone awry...what was suppose to be a simple demonstration has turned into something more...but, don't worry, I got Larry and Bill into this mess, and I'll get them out of it...just bear with me* (turning back to the subjects)...

"Larry...Bill...I see that there are some instructions on this bottle (pretending to read the back of one of the bottles)...*ah...oh...oh...OH, I SEE!....Larry and Bill, there's a simple solution to this problem...It says right here that if I mix these two bottles together, it produces a potion that will absolutely, positively return you both to your original ages...Here, I'm blending the two bottles together* (mixing one into the other, and back again, with equal amounts of liquid left in each bottle)...*youth is mixed with old age and old age is mixed with youth....DRINK!* (handing one bottle to Larry)...*DRINK!* (handing the other bottle to Bill)...*see, ladies and gentlemen...IT'S WORKING...Larry and Bill are both returning to their original ages...when I count to three, you will both be your exact ages as when we started...back to your exact right age... ONE... TWO...THREE!"*

Attack of Amnesia

Facing the audience, *"We've all seen movies where some victim of an accident loses all ability to remember...they fall prey to something we call amnesia...Imagine, for a moment, if you will, that you've had an accident and bumped your head...the next thing you know, you're in a strange bed, in a strange hospital, in a strange town...and everyone is a stranger...stranger still, YOU are a stranger to YOU...medical science says that amnesia is characterized by a temporary loss of memory...but what if you could NEVER remember your past? What if you NEVER regained your name and your life? That you had ab-so-lute-ly no idea who you were...what your name was...or what your life was all about...Well, we're about to perform a live demonstration, through hypnosis, that will give you a glimpse into this phenomenon...a look at just what it would be like to be an amnesia victim..."*

Identifying one of the volunteers, direct your attention to that person. *"In a few moments, I'm going to wake you, and when I do, you will feel perfectly normal in all respects, but you will find that you have lost your memory...you will have no idea what your name is...you will not remember any of your friends or family...you will have no idea where you live...what your life has been like...or even how you got on this stage this evening... YOUR MIND WILL BE COMPLETELY BLANK...you won't remember names, faces... how you got here or where you are...*

"Until I clap my hands...THE MOMENT I CLAP MY HANDS LIKE THIS (demonstrate), *YOU WILL BE ABLE TO REMEMBER EVERYTHING...THE MOMENT I CLAP MY HANDS, EVERYTHING WILL COME BACK TO YOU INSTANTLY...*

"Remember, in a few moments, I will wake you, and when I do, you will feel perfectly normal in all respects, but you will find that you have lost your memory...you will have no idea what your name is...you will not remember any of your friends or family...you will have no idea where you live...what your life has been like...or even how you got on this stage this evening... YOUR MIND WILL BE COMPLETELY BLANK...you won't remember names, faces...how you got here or where you are...

"...I'm going to wake you now, and when I do, you will feel refreshed, renewed, full of energy...feeling wonderful about yourself and everything that's happened to you...but you will find that you have lost your memory...you will have no idea what your name is...you will not remember any of your friends or family...you will have no idea where you live...what your life has been like...or even how you got on this stage this evening...YOUR MIND WILL BE COMPLETELY BLANK....YET, THE MOMENT I CLAP MY HANDS, YOU WILL INSTANTLY BE ABLE TO REMEMBER EVERYTHING...finally, after you awaken, you will be unaware I have told you all of this, and of my telling you this now...okay, here we go...one...two...three...four, starting to wake...five... six...waking up more....seven...eight... waking...NINE... TEN...AWAKE!"

As the subject wakes, bring this person to the front, center stage (let's say it is Debbie), *"Well, hello there. How are you?"* The subject should respond something like, "Fine." *"I'd like to ask you to tell the members of our audience who you are. Would you do that for us?"* The subject is puzzled and uneasy as she tries to think of an answer. *"Just a name will do..."* Still nothing. *"Come on, all I'm asking for is your name...well, if you can't tell us that, how about telling us where you're from?...How about telling me where you are NOW?"* The subject, bewildered, can't answer. *"Please, try hard...think...what's your name...where are you from...can you recall anything about your life...what's your favorite color?..."*

To your assistants backstage, *"Bring out that dressing mirror, would you?"* As they roll it out (or you could simply have a hand mirror nearby), *"Now, I'm going to ask you to look into this mirror and tell me who you see...*(make certain to position the mirror so as not to block the audience's view)...*Hummmm...young lady, I want you to take a seat over here for just a minute or two...I think I know how to clear up this mystery..."*

Place Debbie back to sleep by snapping your fingers and saying *"SLEEP...deep, deep sleep...deeper, deeper...and when you awake, you will feel perfectly normal in all respects, but you will continue to have no idea what your name is...you will not remember any of your friends or family...you will have no idea where you live...what your life has been like...or even how you got on this stage this evening... YOUR MIND WILL BE COMPLETELY BLANK...you won't remember names, faces...how you got here or where you are..."*

Walking over to one of the male subjects, *"When you wake, you are Sigmund Freud, the famous German psychiatrist....when you wake, you are Sigmund Freud...you look like Sigmund Freud, you walk like Sigmund Freud, you speak with that pronounced German accent...YOU ARE SIGMUND FREUD, THE MOST FAMOUS PSYCHIATRIST IN THE WORLD...THE Sigmund Freud..And the woman I'm about to introduce you to has an interesting problem. Physically she is perfectly fine...mentally, she has lost all memory of who she is...but, YOU ARE SIGMUND FREUD, THE MOST FAMOUS PSYCHIATRIST IN THE WORLD...you know that she is the Queen of England...one of your famous patients...and that she suffers from post-hyperamnesia, caused by her rich diet...you will try to talk her back into remembering her identity...*

"...I'm going to wake you now, and when I do, you ARE SIGMUND FREUD, THE MOST FAMOUS PSYCHIATRIST IN THE WORLD...THE Sigmund Freud, psychiatrist extraordinare...you know that this woman you are about to met is really the Queen of England...one of your famous patients...and you will try to talk her back into remembering her identity...finally, after you wake, you will be unaware I have told you all of this, and of my telling you this now...okay, here we go...one...two... three...four, starting to wake...five... six...waking up more....seven... eight... waking...NINE... TEN...AWAKE!"

Speaking with the male subject, *"Hello there, Doctor Sigmund Freud, THE MOST FAMOUS PSYCHIATRIST IN THE WORLD, am I correct?"* "Yes, I'm Sigmund Freud." *"Dr. Freud, or should I call you Sigmund?..."* "Call me Dr. Freud." *"Dr. Freud, I'd like to introduce you to a woman who you might be able to help...she can't remember her name, or anything about herself...* (bringing him over to Debbie)...*Dr. Sigmund Freud, I'd like you to meet...ahh...ahh..."*

By now, he has either chimed in with "The Queen of England," as he launches into his psychoanalysis, or you can prompt the answers. After a few minutes of this, depending on how the conversation is going between the two of them -- and you may need to encourage them at times -- break off the discussion, by asking "Sigmund" to speak to you in the corner. Before you do, though, place Debbie back to sleep.

When you two go off to the corner, *"Dr. Freud, I'm afraid this is a difficult case...even for you...wouldn't you agree?....May I make a suggestion... let me talk to this young lady and see if I can get anywhere with her...* (putting the subject back to sleep) *Sleep...deep, deep, sleep, remember, when you wake, you will still be Doctor Sigmund Freud, the most famous psychiatrist in the world."*

Going back to Debbie and waking her, say, *"Can you believe that guy...the nerve...pretending to be Sigmund Freud, Doctor Sigmund Freud, THE MOST FAMOUS PSYCHIATRIST IN THE WORLD. Listen, we've got to play along with this guy...let's see exactly what he's up to...when I bring him over, you pretend to be the Queen of England..."*

I want to point out an obvious fact: a lot of how the dialogue goes, of how the direction you allow the routine to take, will depend on the responses of the participants. If they are identifying with their characters, if they are playing their roles with eagerness, if they are getting the right audience reaction, leave things alone. If not, you need to prompt them, to move the routine along. Remember one of the first rules of stage hypnotism is to entertain the audience. What's happening on stage not only has to be working as planned, it has to keep the attention of the audience. That means it has to be both interesting and fast-paced.

When a routine is working just "right," give the players room to move. If your subjects take it in a different direction, but it's getting a positive reaction, run with it. When it's not working, and the people are not responding as expected, cut your losses, shorten the routine up, and move on to something else.

Bringing Debbie and "Dr. Freud" back to center stage, *"Dr. Freud, I've had a discussion with your patient, and I think you'll find she is very willing to speak with you now...Miss, you are ready to admit you are the Queen of England, aren't you?"*

At this point, the two subjects should be into their parts. If they are, let it proceed for a few minutes. If it's not going as planned, try injecting ideas. Either way, after a few minutes, say, *"Queen...Dr. Freud...SLEEP! Deep...deep. sleep...(have them sit)...I want you both to sleep...drifting deeper and deeper...d-e-e-p-e-r and d-e-e-p-e-r...and when I wake you, you Dr. Freud, will no longer be Dr. Freud...YOU WILL BE THE QUEEN OF ENGLAND...that's right, when I awaken you, you Dr. Freud, will no longer be Dr. Freud...YOU WILL BE THE QUEEN OF ENGLAND...*

"...and young lady, when I wake you, you will no longer be the Queen of England...YOU WILL BE Doctor Sigmund Freud, THE MOST FAMOUS PSYCHIATRIST IN THE WORLD...that's right, when I wake you...YOU WILL BE DOCTOR SIGMUND FREUD, THE MOST FAMOUS PSYCHIATRIST IN THE WORLD...okay, here we go...one...two... three...four, starting to wake...five... six...waking up more....seven...eight... waking... NINE... TEN...AWAKE!"

This introduces a remarkable juxtaposition of characters. The Queen is now Freud, and Freud is now the Queen. Additionally, you have a male subject acting in a female role, and visa versa.

When the subjects awaken, you want to let them carry the conversation, let them play out their new-found roles. When you're ready to break off the routine, gain the attention of both subjects and clap your hands, saying, *"You are both now back as yourselves, everything is normal...Debbie, you now remember your name and everything about your life...(to the male subject) You now remember your name and everything about your life."*

Trip To Pluto

Gather up everyone but one subject. Leave him off in the corner for now. Tell everyone else they are about to meet a real, honest-to-goodness space alien. *"When all of you wake, I have a big surprise for you...we are all about to meet a genuine space alien...his name is Mooky, and he is from Pluto. He has traveled millions of miles through outer space to be here tonight...so when you all wake, I will ask our visitor to join us...one small detail, though...Mooky doesn't speak English, or any language on Earth, for that matter...he only speaks Plutonese...But fortunately (picking one of the subjects) Debbie can speak Plutonese...(directing your commands to her) Debbie, when you wake, you will find that you can understand and speak Plutonese and will act as the translator for our group...whatever our outer space friend says, you will translate into English, and then when we want to say something to Mooky, you will translate it back into Plutonese..."*

To Debbie *"Remember, Debbie in a few moments, I will wake you, and when I do, you will feel perfectly normal in all respects, but you will find that you can understand and speak Plutonese and will act as the translator for our group...whatever our outer space friend says, you will translate to English, and then when we want to say something to Mooky, you will translate it back into Plutonese..."*

Now give your suggestions to the subject who was asked to wait in the corner. *"When you wake, you will be Mooky, the friendly space alien from Pluto...you have come millions of miles to visit the planet Earth on a mission of peace...Pluto is a lovely planet, but you have almost no women...you want a few women who would like to come back to Pluto...that is your mission...you cannot speak English... you speak only Plutonese., but Debbie speaks both English and Plutonese and will translate for you..*

"Remember, I will wake you, and when I do, YOU will be Mooky, the friendly space alien from Pluto...here to convince women to come back to Pluto with you...you cannot speak English... you speak only Plutonese...

"Okay, I'm going to wake you all now...here we go...one...two... three...four, starting to wake...five...six...waking up more....seven...eight...waking... NINE...TEN... AWAKE!..."

As they wake, *"Members of the committee and those of you in the audience...I have a big surprise for you...tonight you will meet a real space alien...Mooky, from the planet Pluto...while Mooky doesn't speak any Earth language, we are fortunate, because one of our committee members, Debbie, does...she will do all the translating for us...*

"Debbie, would you ask Mooky to please step forward, and as he does, ladies and gentlemen, let's give him a warm, warm Earth welcome by applauding..."

Debbie should be inventing and speaking some gibberish to communicate with our space friend. If not, you will need to prompt her on. As she calls Mooky over and he comes down to center stage, start applauding, if the audience hasn't already.

"Debbie, please tell our visitor we welcome him to Earth and that we hope he has come in peace...(she does, and Mooky, in turn, gives her his gibberish back)...What did he say? (she'll probably respond something about his mission being peaceful)..."

"Debbie, ask him why he has come to Earth...(as she does, and he responds, and she translates, the plot should unfold as you outlined it earlier to the subjects. If not, you need to direct it that way)..."

Other questions to follow should lead to a sexual interplay between Debbie and Mooky. Because Debbie is, in theory translating only what Mooky says, she can afford to be frank and honest. We will use this to our comic advantage. Here are some questions to have asked.

"Debbie, ask Mooky what kind of woman he is looking for?" The answers usually come back with things like big-breasted, very sexy, etc.

"Debbie, ask Mooky if they have sex on Pluto, and if they do, is it any different than the way we do it on earth?"

"Debbie, ask Mooky what he thinks is the best thing about Earth women?"

"Debbie, would you consider returning to Pluto with Mooky?"

When you've gotten the reaction you're looking for, you can put everyone back to sleep and remove the suggestion, or you can try something else. Here's one idea.

"I have another surprise for our committee members...we're are about to take a trip back to Pluto in Mooky's space ship...I want you all to close your eyes

now...everyone close your eyes until I tell you to open them...and when you do, you will find yourself in the space ship...all right, you can open your eyes now...

"*Well, we're in Mooky's space ship...isn't it fantastic?...Okay, we're taking off...we're lifting off...can you all feel the pressure?...we're going up, and up, and up....faster and faster...we're in outer space ....outside of Earth's gravitational pull...the pressure is off your body...you feel fine now...as we are hurdling at a million miles a minute towards Pluto...look out the windows... there's Mars!* (pointing)*...now we're passing Saturn...look at all the stars...it's almost like you can reach out and touch them* (gesturing)*...we're slowing down...we're coming in for a landing...better buckle those seat belts...Pluto isn't known for having the best runways...*(bouncing up and down)*...boom!... we're down...we've landed...WE'RE ON PLUTO.*"

For a little comic relief, have a female assistant off-stage say over the public address system, "*Ladies and Gentlemen, welcome to Pluto...this is the conclusion of flight 999 on PlutoAir, the number one airline in the galaxy...In a moment, we will be opening the space door and you may exit the space ship...the air on Pluto is the same as Earth...But, watch out...our gravity is very weak...you may feel as though you are floating in slow motion...just like you're walking on clouds...that's normal on Pluto...enjoy your stay on Pluto, or wherever your final destination may be, and remember that the next time you're flying in outer space, think of PlutoAir...Our motto is WE'RE OUTTA THIS WORLD!*"

As you take over again, "*All right everyone, let's exit the space ship and take a look around...*(herding up everyone and leading them out the "door", bringing them together at one end of the stage, with you, Mooky and Debbie in front)*...Debbie, would you ask Mooky to show us around?...*(again, rather than try to script this, let these two subjects create the walking tour).*"

When you're done, end the routine this way, "*Okay, folks...it's time to return to Earth...Mooky would you guide us back?...Everyone please re-enter the space ship and take your seats* (leading people back through the "door")*...if you would all put your seat belts on, and close your eyes we'll prepare to lift-off...here we go...ten...nine...eight...seven...six...five.. .four...three...two...one... BLAST OFF!...we're in outer space...eyes closed... until I tell you you can open them...this time, we'll take a short cut...we're almost back on Earth...we're slowing down...we're landing...WE'VE LANDED!...You can open your eyes now...we are back where we started...*(taking Mooky aside, remove the suggestion).*"

Three-Ring Circus

Choosing three members of the committee, let's say they are Jane, Bill and Mark, give them their individual instructions:

"*Tonight, you three people are circus performers...you are all part of a circus that has come to town, and will put on a fabulous show on this stage ...*"

Speaking to each person individually, "*Jane, you are Jane the Magnificent, a high-wire performer. You will perform on the high-wire and impress the entire audience...you will be great!...Bill, you are Bill the Clown, the world's greatest juggling clown. You will juggle several balls at one time...And Mark, you have a trained dog show, you are Mark and his Dynamic Dogs, and you will perform for us tonight* (turning to the audience)...

"Ladies and gentlemen...we're proud to bring to you this evening, the world's greatest circus, Bumbling Brothers Big Top Circus. In the far ring is Jane the Magnificent, high-wire walker extraordinare. Jane will perform her death-defying act 50 feet above the sawdust floor, without a net! Let's have a big hand for Jane the Magnificent...In the center circle, we are pleased to bring you, all the way from (Bill's real hometown), *Bill the Clown. Bill will amaze you with his juggling skills. Bill is the only person alive today that can juggle SIX balls at once...as you're about to see...and in the last ring, we have Mark and his dynamic trained dogs. Mark and his canine pals have been delighting audiences throughout Europe, and we're very happy they are making their U.S. debut on this stage...let's give a big hand to all of them...*

"And so, without further ado, here they are, Jane, Bill, and Mark...Maestro...a drum roll...spot light on Jane...as she climbs the rope to her high wire perch waaaay up (pointing to the ceiling) *there...*

"Let's cheer Jane on....Bill, let's see that juggling magic at work...folks, with your applause, show Bill how great a job he is doing...and Mark, we're ready for your trained dogs to perform..."

You can keep this routine up for a few minutes and end it, or add more. For example, as the performers are playing their parts, you can employ other subjects to fill out the show. One subject can be told he is the popcorn vendor, and is to go among the audience selling his wares, *"Hur-ray...hur-ray, get your popcorn...hot dogs...soda...one dol-lar...Hur-ray...hur-ray, get you popcorn...hot dogs...soda... one dol-lar..."*

Another can be the side-show barker. You may want to give him a script to read, like this, *"Ladies and gentlemen, children of all ages, step right up...because behind this tent are some of the seven wonders of the world...see a three-headed dog...see Elmo the elephant boy with ears as big as Dumbo...see Serina the Snake Woman...her skin will drive you out of your skin...see Jumbo Jake, the tallest man in the world...and don't forget to see, with your very own eyes...live...without trick mirrors or special devices,, The Amazon Woman who will turn into a gorilla -- as you watch...hurray, hur-ray, hur-ray, only one dol-lar...ten dimes...four thin quarters...the show's about to start..."*

Two Great Finales: The Human Bridge And The Ring of Fire

Now you're ready to perform a sensational routine or two that give a strong finish to the show. Here are a couple that fill that bill.

THE HUMAN BRIDGE

In this routine, a subject is placed across two chairs, without any support in the middle, and you stand up on the person's outstretched body.

Choose one of your best subjects. Because of the physical nature of this routine, if you pick a small-statured person, ideally a woman, the effects are much more dramatic. Let's say this is Mary. (Please make sure the subject has no physical impairments, such as a bad back that would potentially harm her).

"Folks, we're about to do something that will appear to be impossible. In a few moments, I will suspend Mary across these two chairs, with no supports or hidden wires...her body will remain stretched across the chairs...at which point, I will stand on top of her with the full weight of my body...watch and be amazed!"

Take the subject to a corner of the stage. Having her stand erect, with her feet together, *"Mary, eyes closed...deep, deep sleep... I want you allow yourself to drift off into a deep, deep sleep...I want you to go deep, deep to sleep...and as you drift off deeper, I want you to feel every muscle in your body becoming rigid, growing stiff and hard...*(as you press on the person shoulders) *I want you to feel your back and shoulders becoming rigid...every muscle in your body, from your top to your toes are getting stiff, rigid, STIFF and RIGID...it's as though a steel rod is running through your body...your body is becoming AS STIFF AND RIGID AS A STEEL BAR...AS STIFF AND RIGID AS A STEEL BAR..."*

(Pressing on her arms, moving your hands down from the shoulders to the fingers, and pressing on her back and stomach -- all the time checking for rigidity) *"As I pass my hands across you, you can feel your body stiff and rigid...every single muscle in your body is completely stiff...AS STIFF AND RIGID AS A STEEL BAR...You cannot move a muscle in your body...nothing can make you bend...NOTHING CAN MAKE YOU BEND...YOUR BODY IS AS STIFF AND RIGID AS A STEEL BAR...AS STIFF AND RIGID AS A STEEL BAR...NOTHING CAN MAKE YOU BEND!"*

You'll need a couple of assistants (these can be spectators) to help you lift the person up onto the two chairs, placing her shoulders across the back of one chair, and her legs, in the middle of her calves, across the back of the other chair. You may want to use upholstered chairs, or place some kind of padding or a pillow on the top of the chairs to make it more comfortable for the subject.

Turning to the audience, *"I am now going to place Mary across these two chairs...*(while helping place her gently on the chairs whisper to Mary that she is stiff and rigid -- repeating this as she is placed across the chairs).*"* The subject's back should be arched upward if they are fully rigid. If not, give her more suggestions. By the way, anyone, whether hypnotized or not, if they remain in this rigid position, can support the weight of someone standing on them. It's another physiological trick.

"With the help of my able-bodied assistants, I will now stand on Mary, placing the full weight of my body on her stomach..." Have a few assistants help you to plant your feet on the subject. You may want to use a small ladder to help in this effort, having it removed, to avoid having the audience think it is rigged to hold you up. Position your feet such that one foot is just below the chest, or on a man, on his chest, and the other on the middle of the thigh. You may want to have one or two people hold your hand to keep your balance as you adjust your feet. Once in position, don't move or shift your weight.

"Ladies and gentlemen, as you can see with your own two eyes, all ___ pounds of my body are being held up by this young lady...proving the power of the mind to do the seemingly impossible."

After a few moments, grab the hand of a waiting assistant and leap off the subject onto the floor, and say, *"Let's give Mary a big hand!"*

Right now, the subject is in a deep trance. You will need to bring her back. Turning to her, have two assistants help you lower her from the chairs. You must then tell her, *"Mary, your body is no longer rigid...every muscle in your body is beginning to relax...your body is no longer stiff...all the stiffness is gone...and in a moment when I wake you, you will feel wonderful...your body is no longer stiff...all the stiffness is gone...on the count of ten you will awake, feeling perfectly fine...one...stiffness disappearing...two...three...feeling good...four...five...six...feeling wonderful...seven... eight...waking up...NINE...almost awake...TEN, AWAKE!"*

PLEASE NOTE: This routine and the one that follows involve an element of danger. Anytime you stand on a person, whether hypnotized or not, you chance injuring that individual. Obviously, if you stand squarely on the person's stomach you can put extreme pressure on the back. Standing with your feet apart, one above the stomach and one on the thigh area helps, although it doesn't eliminate the possibility of injury. In the Ring of Fire routine that follows, since you are using real fire, you need to be very careful to insure that the subject is not put in too much danger. Moreover, anytime you use fire in an enclosed structure you need to take fire safety precautions, like having an assistant standing by with a fire extinguisher at the ready.

THE RING OF FIRE

We now end our routines with panache! Choosing one of your best subjects (say it's Mark), an athletic subject who seems nimble, have your assistant(s) roll the "Ring of Fire" on stage. This can be a three-foot (or wider) metal ring you fabricate, attached to an 18-inch square wooden base that has been weighted down for support. Or you can nail a store-bought plastic hoola hoop to a wooden box. With either one, I'd suggest using a flammable material that is relatively easy to contain, like rubber cement (used in many movie special effects). Avoid gasoline or other highly combustible substances! You'll also need a mat for the person to tumble onto, like an exercise mat, air cushion or a mattress.

"If I can direct everyone's attention to the object being brought out on stage. I call it the 'Ring of Fire.' In a minute, you will witness something spectacular, something that will have you on the edge of your chairs, something that will have you holding your breath...a test of courage...a test of F-I-R-E!...as I light this hoop on fire, sending gigantic flames shooting skyward through the air...and when the fire is at its peak, when the temperature is hot enough to melt your socks (taking your hand and pointing to the subject, who, at this point, probably looks quite nervous).*.Mark will leap through the Ring of Fire...unharmed!"* You want to deliver this with a little bit of humor to break the ice.

A few notes on this stunt. First of all, if prepared the right way, there is virtually no danger involved. It may look spectacular to the audience, but the subject is very safe. You do need to take special measures, though. First of all, the Ring should be sturdily made. You should take reasonable precautions, like having a couple of assistants standing by with fire extinguishers, and using fire resistant materials around the Ring.

"Mark, I have all the confidence in the world you'll not only be able to meet this challenge, but it could be the start of a whole new career...(putting the subject to sleep)*...Sleep Mark...deep, deep sleep...drifting off deeper, and deeper, and d-e-e-p-e-r to sleep...Mark, when you wake, you will be Mark the Man of Fire, Mark, the man afraid of nothing...you will leap through this ring with the greatest of ease, tumbling through and landing on the mat on the other side...Mark, you are Mark the Man of Fire...you will tumble through the Ring and do it perfectly...we will practice a few times without the ring on fire...you will do it just as I demonstrate...you will do it perfectly...each time...in a few moments I will wake you and you will be Mark the Man of Fire...you will leap through the flaming Ring of Fire perfectly...you will be great!...*

"Okay, I'm going to wake you now...here we go...one...two... three...four, starting to wake...five... six...waking up more....seven...eight... waking... NINE...TEN...AWAKE!...

"Ladies and gentlemen, a big hand for the star of our show, Mark the Man of Fire!...Yes!...isn't he wonderful...(encouraging the applause)*...Mark, I'm going to let you practice this death-defying stunt by having you leap through the ring before I light it on fire..."*

Instruct the subject on how to leap through the Ring, with his hands directly out in front of him and touching each other, and to tumble onto the mat on the other side. Have him try this a few times until he is very confident. Again, do this a few times until he is sure of his ability.

With the subject ready and confident, turn to the audience, *"We're about to light the 'Ring of Fire'...we are about to send Mark hurdling through the flaming fires...of having him risk life and limb simply for our viewing pleasure...just kidding Mark!...Seriously folks, Mark will attempt near certain death - - - defying abilities to challenge the Ring of Fire!...let's all show him how much we appreciate what he's about to do..."*

The idea here is to excite the crowd and build up the suspense. The trick itself only lasts a few seconds. So, we want to make it seem worthwhile.

Turning back to our subject, *"Okay Mark, the big moment has arrived...are you ready?....Good!...here we go...assistant, please light the Ring of Fire...drum roll please Maestro...*(play the soundtrack of a drum roll)*...Mark, on the count of three, you will leap through the Ring of Fire... ONE...ready... TWO...set to go...THREE...GO!"*

As he lands on the other side, rush over to help him up, as your assistants use the fire extinguishers they are holding to put out the ring of fire. Holding up his hand in your hand say, *"There you are...Mark the Man of Fire has successfully challenged and conquered the Ring of Fire!"*

The Finish

Here's a great way to finish your act. Turning to your subjects say, *"You've all been excellent subjects to work with this evening...I hope you've enjoyed yourselves as much as we've enjoyed having you...*

"In a moment I'm going to wake you for the last time...and when I do, you will feel refreshed, renewed...full of new-found energy...but, as I ask you to leave the stage and return to your seats, you will discover that the floor is very sticky...and as you try to walk...your feet will feel like there is a gooey, gooey glue-like substance on the bottom of your shoes...and it will make every step you take very tough...like you're in slow motion, walking on the moon...and once off the stage, you'll find that you can walk quite normally, and you will then proceed directly to your chair...

"All right, here we go...ONE you're sleeping deeply, but now it's time to get up...TWO... beginning to wake up...THREE...FOUR...feeling very good...FIVE...SIX...waking up more...SEVEN... eight...waking...NINE...TEN...(snapping your finger) *AWAKE!..."*

As the subjects awake, turning to the audience and then back to the volunteers say, *"Folks, let's give our volunteers a big, big round of applause for being such good sports and doing such a good job...aren't they wonderful...and now I will ask you all, if you will, to please return to your seats in the audience..."*

Naturally as they try to move across the stage, they find that their feet are very sticky, and they will struggle to get off the stage. This makes for a great ending, as you add, *"And so ladies and gentlemen of the audience, and esteemed members of the committee who have been kind enough to help in our demonstrations, I thank you all and hope you find the experience interesting and exciting. I did! Again, thank you all."* Bowing to the audience, you exit the stage.

A Couple of Afterthoughts

When preparing your subjects for a routine, be very specific in giving instructions. Tell them in as much detail as possible what you expect of them. Some subjects are creative and imaginative and need little direction. Others, however, need you to paint the picture for them.

If you find yourself with too many subjects on stage at one time, you might want to try this: identifying one or more subjects you'd like to dismiss, yet be able to call back up on stage, tell them *"When you wake, I will ask you to return to your seat in the audience, and as you do, the moment you sit down, you will instantly fall asleep, gently placing your head on the table* (or, *in your lap,* if there is no table)...*and will remain asleep until I tell you otherwise."*

Another thing to keep in mind is that not all subjects are able to outwardly express themselves like you would want. Some are great pantominists and can pretend anything. Others have difficulty, even though they may inwardly accept the suggestion. Use subjects who display animated skills for the more visual experiments.

Finally, it is common for people to disbelieve that they have been hypnotized the first time it occurs, because the hypnotic feeling is not a completely unique feeling. It is something that may feel familiar to them. Situations where a subject responds perfectly to all suggestions, and yet, when awakened, insists that he was never hypnotized, are common. The rationale is usually, "I was conscious all the time, I knew what I was doing, and I could have stopped anytime I wanted. I just didn't want to"

One way to "solve" this problem is to induce amnesia at the end of your show. Just before you wake everyone up for the last time, tell them, *"In a moment, when I wake you, you will feel wonderful...you will feel very good...but you will have no memory whatsoever of what occurred on this stage tonight...It will feel as though you just dozed off for a few minutes and then awoke...and if anyone talks to you about things you supposedly did on stage, you will think that they are trying to put you on...Again, when you wake, you will feel wonderful...but you will have no memory whatsoever of what occurred on this stage tonight..."*

Ten More Stage Routines

To add spice to your act, here are ten more ideas for routines:

1. MADONNA

Tell a subject that when she awakens, she will be a famous singer, like Madonna. *"When you wake, you will find that you are the famous rock and roll singer Madonna* (or whomever you choose, or in the case of a male subject, a male singer, like Michael Jackson), *and you will perform live for us tonight on this stage..."* As she's waking up, say, *"Ladies and gentlemen, I'm extremely pleased to advise you that Madonna, one of the greatest singers alive today is on our stage...here she is...Madonna...and with further ado, let's hear her live, now...Madonna, it's all yours...*(as you say this, turn on a Madonna record and hand the subject a microphone)*...".*

To add spice to this routine, select one or more subjects, handing them paper and pencils, and instruct them that they are big, big fans of Madonna, and when she finishes singing, they are suppose to go over and ask her for an autograph.

2. GIVE ME A HUG

Using a female subject say, *"When you wake, you will feel perfectly normal in every respect, except that whenever I say the word, 'hasenpfeffer,' you will have an uncontrollable urge to come over and give me the biggest, most sensual hug you can...and that's exactly what you will do...you will rush right over and give me a big hug...again, anytime I say the word, 'hasenpfeffer,' you will have an uncontrollable urge to come over and give me the biggest, most sensual hug you can...and the more I say the word hasenpfeffer,' the more you will hug me..."*

This is a great gimmick to use early in the show. Give this command, and every so often, after a routine, or in the middle of one, say *"hasenpfeffer,"* and watch the reaction!

3. MALE STRIPPER

To a male subject say, *"When you wake, you will be* (let's say his name is Henry) *Henry the Hunk, the sexiest male stripper at Chippendales...you will be performing your strip tease tonight for an audience of woman attending a female bachelorette party...they've come a long way to see you strut your stuff...and you're not about to disappoint them...because, you are HENRY THE HUNK, THE SEXIEST MALE STRIPPER AROUND...OKAY, HENRY, GET READY TO DO YOUR MOST SENSUOUS STRIP TEASE...ready, to wake? ...here we go..."*

Once awake, say, *"Ladies, we're pleased to present for your viewing enjoyment, the world's sexiest male stripper, the man that has the body of a god and the gyrations of Michael Jackson...here he is...and let's give him a big round of applause, Henry the Hunk...Henry, show these ladies E-V-E-R-Y-T-H-I-N-G YOU'VE GOT!...*(as you put on the theme song from *Gypsy*).

Some men will actually start to remove their clothes in a real strip tease. Others will only imitate taking their clothes off. If the subject does start to strip, be sure to not let it go too far.

4. THE WAITER

Tell one of the subjects that he is a waiter at club (or wherever you are performing) and he is to go out among the crowd and solicit drink orders.

"When you wake, you will a waiter in this club...you will go out to the audience, and going from table to table, you will ask people what they would like to drink, and write it down with this pencil, using this pad of paper. (hand both to the subject)*..remember, you are a waiter in this club...you will go out to the audience and ask people what they would like to drink..."*

To add a nice touch, you might want to dress your subject up in a waiter's outfit, complete with the bar towel slung across the arm.

5. WHO WEARS THE PANTS IN THE FAMILY?

Tell a married female subject that when she wakes up, she will be very annoyed with her husband's clothing, and will proceed to berate him for being so unfashionable.

"When you wake, you will look over at your husband, only to discover that he looks disheveled, and is dressed like a nerd...and it's embarrassing...you will then proceed to lecture him on how he should dress...and when you talk to him, don't hold back...really tell him off for being such a slob...but, any time I point my finger at you and say, 'time out,' you will be frozen in place, and unable to speak. or move a muscle...until I tell you otherwise."

After awakening the subject and she begins yelling at her poor husband, point and say, *"Time out."*

6. MAKE UP YOUR MIND

Tell a subject that after he wakes, he will rush back to his seat in the audience, and immediately upon sitting down, will fall fast asleep...until you snap your fingers, at which time he will wake up, and dash back on stage to take the seat he has now. When he sits down, he will fall deep, deep asleep.

"When you wake, you will immediately rush back to your seat in the audience and sit down...and the minute you are seated, you will instantly fall deep, deep asleep...and you will remain asleep until I snap my fingers and say, 'Now!'...at which time you will wake and rush back on stage as quickly as you can and take your seat...as soon as you do, you will instantly fall asleep...fast, fast asleep..."

7. FIRST DATE

Choosing a male and female subject (let's say it's Debbie and Mark), tell them that when they open their eyes, they are both 16-year olds and out on their first date. Having them sit side-by-side, tell them, *"You're having a wonderful time on your first date...you went to a fabulous restaurant, had a wonderful meal, then saw an excellent movie...now you're in Mark's car, parked in a secluded spot, and you can see the city lights in the darkness...it's very, very romantic...Mark, you think Debbie looks beautiful and she smells r-e-a-l- good...it's turning you on...you'd like to kiss her, but you're a little shy...Debbie, you think Mark is handsome and smart...he's been a perfect gentleman, too...you're having a wonderful time, and want him to kiss you, but you don't want to say anything that might make him believe you are being too aggressive...when you both awake...you'll be in the car...looking out over the city lights...Mark, you will ask Debbie to describe how she liked the movie you two just saw...it was a romantic movie, where the handsome prince falls in love with the beautiful servant girl and they have a romantic encounter...Debbie, you'll be trying to let Mark know, though subtle hints that you'd like him to kiss you...to kiss you as passionately as the lovers in the movie... you will do this by describing what you saw of the movie and trying to let Mark know that you'd love to be kissed that way, too...Mark, as Debbie describes the scene in the movie where the lovers meet in some secluded spot, watching the lights of the city...you will get very turned on by this...as will you Debbie...and you'll find yourselves soon in a passionate embrace."*

8. ROSES ARE RED

Tell all the female subjects that they are in a beautiful garden, a rose garden, and they are to pick the roses, and then go out in the audience, giving a flower to each man they see that they find attractive, and to give him a kiss on the cheek.

"When you open your eyes, you will find yourselves in a beautiful rose garden. The place smells so good...they're are all kinds of roses...red roses...pink roses...white roses...and these roses DON'T have thorns that can prick you...As you gather up the roses, picking as many as you'd like, smell their wonderful scent...and when you're done picking the flowers, I want each one of you to go into the audience and hand a rose to each man you see that you're attracted to...as you hand him the rose, say, 'A kiss on the cheek for this rose'...and then give him a big hung and kiss on the cheek..."

9. CATCH ANY FISH LATELY?

Here's a running gag you can use through the entire show. Early on, take a subject aside and hand him a stick or broom handle with two feet of string attached, have him sit on a chair, and place a pail of water in front of him.

"When you wake, you will be at a lake...fishing...you have your fishing pole in your hand and the lake is in front of you...the first thing you need to do is bait your hook, then, put your pole in the water...watch out for fish stealing your bait...you may want to check your pole every few minutes. When you catch a fish, put it in a pile by the side of your chair."

10. THE HINDU ROPE TRICK

Here's an old favorite of stage hypnotists. Suggest to the group, *"I have one more surprise for you today, we are all going on a trip to India, where the famous Swami Salami will perform his Hindu Rope trick...I want everyone to close their eyes...and when I tell you to open them, we will be magically transported back to India...*

"Okay, you can open your eyes...We are in India!...and there (pointing) *is the Swami himself...watch closely...he's coming over this way...he is bowing to us now...let us all bow back to him...Watch that large rope he has in his hand...LOOK, HE'S TOSSING IT UP IN THE AIR* (as you look upward) *AND IT REMAINS HANGING IN THE AIR!...Wow, I've never seen anything like it...*

"Now the Swami is bringing out a small boy...the boy is grabbing the rope...now he is climbing up the rope...higher and higher...and higher...he's so high now, I can't see him...the boy has vanished into thin air!...

"The Swami is now calling the boy down...but he is not coming...he keeps calling...but the boy does not respond...the Swami tugs on the rope...harder...HARDER...the rope crashes to ground...but the boy is gone!...

"Now two assistants are bringing a big straw basket...and several large swords...the Swami stabs the swords into the basket...first one...then another...and another...four.. .five...six...seven...EIGHT GIANT SWORDS HAVE BEEN THRUST THROUGH THAT BASKET...now he is withdrawing all those swords...three left...two left...he's pulling out the last one...

"The lid on the basket is moving...and basket is shaking...it's tipping over!...the lid has fallen off...AND THE LITTLE BOY IS EMERGING FROM THE BASKET...THAT IS AMAZING! The boy is inside the basket...HE'S COMING OUT!...THAT'S AMAZING!...

"What a phenomenal trick...let's give Swami Salami a big, big hand (start applauding)...*Okay...it's time to travel back home...close your eyes...when I tell you to open them...you'll be back on the stage where we started from...All right, we're back now, you can open your eyes..."*

Stage Preparation

When you plan your show, the scenery, props, lighting, and music, can add to the enjoyment of the performance.

The props in hypnotism are few. The chairs used should be simple, straight-back chairs without arms. They should be set up in a semi-circle. Depending on the size of the stage and the audience, half-a-dozen to a dozen chairs are ideal. If you get more volunteers on stage than you have chairs, have the extra people stand directly behind the chairs.

At the beginning of the show, when you are trying to produce conditions favorable for induction, you want the lights dimmed and the music, if any, very low. Once the subjects are hypnotized, they should be unfazed by external disturbances, so lights and music can be turned up.

Some routines can be made more interesting and exciting through the use of special props and sound effects. In the trip to Pluto, having flying saucer sounds and other special effects build the mood.

Five Rules of Stage Hypnotism

1. THE FIRST RULE OF STAGE HYPNOTISM IS TO ENTERTAIN THE AUDIENCE. While it's important to work closely with your subjects on stage and to try to bring out the best in them, the goal here is to entertain the audience. Make that priority number one.

2. WHEN NOT IN ACTION, KEEP SUBJECTS ASLEEP. If you have a group of volunteers on stage and you're only using some in a routine, keep the other hypnotized subjects asleep.

3. KEEP THE ACTION GOING. It's so easy to let a routine continue. But, pacing the show is very important. Keep things moving along. Don't spend a lot of time of any one thing.

4. LEAD THE ORCHESTRA, DON'T PLAY THE INSTRUMENTS. Simply stated, let your subjects be the center of the audience's attention. Direct the action, but don't hog the show.

5. HAVING COMPLETED ONE SERIES OF SUGGESTIONS, ALWAYS REMOVE THEM before presenting any new set of suggestions, or one might conflict with the other.

Chapter

9

Self Hypnosis

You can learn to stop smoking, to diet properly, to quit drinking, to control pain, to better focus your energies, to conquer fears, to name a few.

All *hypnosis*, in reality, is self-hypnosis.

Whether a person is guided or guides himself into the trance state is immaterial. The hypnotized subject is the one allowing everything to happen. It is *his* hypnosis. If a hypnotist, or operator, is involved, that person only acts to facilitate the process.

When it comes to self-hypnosis, *you*, then, are both the bus driver and the passenger. And don't be fooled, there are some amazing and long-lasting beneficial effects you can achieve on your own through self-hypnosis. You can learn to stop smoking, to diet properly, to quit drinking, to control pain, to better focus your energies, to conquer fears, to name a few.

The "secret" behind self-hypnosis is use of posthypnotic suggestions. A posthypnotic suggestion is a suggestion given while a person is in the hypnotic state that calls for action or some response to take place after the hypnotic experience. They are potent extensions, then, of self-hypnosis. They allow you to change or improve your habits and behaviors.

The reason posthypnotic suggestions work is that you have implanted cues in your subconscious mind that provoke an action or response automatically. Let's say, for instance, that you find yourself in a tension-filled environment at work or in a social setting. You can call up your response cue, say it is the action of making a fist and slowly opening your hand, relaxing your muscles, that triggers the internal response to release the tension inside.

One more point to make: posthypnotic suggestions work only if you want them to. You must be motivated, you must be willing to accept the change as it comes.

The Preparation Phase

Before we get into practicing self-hypnosis, there are some preliminary things you need to know and do.

The first, is to select a place to practice. It should be quiet, comfortable, and safe from interfering eyes and any interruptions.

Self-hypnosis takes practice. You don't do it once and put it on a shelf. It's something that you should consider making a part of your regimen, whether that's daily, once a week, or once a month. Initially, you may want to block out 20 to 30 minutes per session. As you become more skilled at entering the trance state, you may find you only need eight to 10 minutes per session to accomplish the same benefits.

Once you've chosen the place, you need to find a relaxed position. Some people prefer lying down, while others may chose to relax upright in a chair. It's up to you. Using plenty of pillows can help, too.

Okay, let's assume you've found your favorite spot, the lights are subdued, and you've settled into a comfortable lounge chair, what's next?

Close your eyes, take a deep breath, breathing in through your nose...hold it for three seconds...and *slowly* exhale through your mouth over a six-second period. Inhale...hold it...exhale...inhale...hold it...exhale. Do this for two minutes. Slow, deep, rhythmic breathing helps you to relax. Imagine your tensions flowing out of you with every bit of air you release.

In this tranquil state, you're ready for your self-hypnosis induction, the second step in the process. You've already finished the first: relaxation. The following script starts out with the "long version" of the induction process, followed by the conditioning statement you add in, depending on which is appropriate (smoking, dieting, pain control, etc.), finishing up with the awakening technique.

I suggest you tape record the script, or have someone with a calm and serene voice tape it for you, to be played back at each session.

Script For The Long Method of Hypnosis

"You're here to take a nap. You're resting comfortably. You're happy to do what you do when you take a nap...forget the rest of the world. Give up the world, and drift off to sleep without care or concern...There is no effort here, it's just comfort and ease...

"There is no trying to take a nap. It's just permission. Permit yourself some calmness, patience, pleasantness, and gentleness. Don't try hard for these things. Permit them in a passing way...

"A second or two of calmness...a second or two of pleasantness...a second or two of gentleness...

"There is no effort or strain involved in these things. Give permission for calmness...give permission for patience...give permission for gentleness...give permission for gentle resolve to feel the feelings I describe to you...

"It's a real good thing we do here today, so let us be pleasant in advance...be patient with me and with yourself...and I will be eternally patient with you...Be gently resolved to feel the feelings I describe to you...

"Those words, 'gently resolved,' are so soft, they're like light, puffy white clouds...

"Also, I would like you to pretend and imagine and make believe. These are not false nor are they false feelings...

"They are creative...You can see this! Think of the novelist or artist...they all pretend...and imagine...and make believe in their creative work...and when this is coupled with their talent and effort, they achieve something of substance, like a novel, or a painting, or an invention...

"So, if I ask you to pretend, or imagine, or make believe, please do it in whatever way is easy and comfortable to you...

"Also, people are great. But most people don't know they are great and may never, even in a lifetime, ask of themselves one moment of greatness...and sadly for them, may never achieve one...

"But I know that people are great and I am constantly amazed at the magnificence of change for the better that results when you go to a person's greatest...their subconscious mind, where your greatness is...

"And so I say to you, in YOUR greatness...you have the beautiful and easy ability to speak to parts of your body...to tell parts of your body what to do...and they will do what it is you tell them...provided you have those nice elements that build a bridge to your inner mind, namely, calmness... patience...pleasantness...and gentleness...

"And likewise, in your greatness, you have the truly magnificent and astonishing ability to speak to parts of your MIND...and those parts of your mind will do what you tell them to do...provided you have those nice elements that build a bridge to your inner mind, namely, calmness... patience...pleasantness...and gentleness...which you now have...

"So, let us permit parts of your body to feel comfortable, good feelings...let us give permission of your head to feel heavy...for your eyelids, though closed, to feel heavy, for your arms to feel heavy...as they rest there, for your legs and body to feel more heavy...

"With every breath you take...in...and out...in...and out...feel your head get heavy...feel your shoulders get heavy...feel your arms get heavy...feel your fingers get heavy...feel your back get heavy...feel your legs get heavy...feel your toes get heavy...feel yourself sinking deeper and deeper...visualize your tension flowing out of you...

"You welcome every feeling of comfort...and ease...and heaviness...and this is identical to the floating feeling you experience in the twilight of sleep...where you can hardly reach over to turn off a night lamp or to put aside a magazine or book you've been reading...

"This heaviness is not added weight...rather the heaviness you feel comes from the beautiful loosening of your muscles...welcome this heaviness wherever it comes to you...

"And now let's pretend...let's imagine...let's make-believe...

"Let's make believe you live in a little country town, by a beautiful river, near a mountain...it's a warm summer day...you pack a picnic...let's head down this mountain trail...you've got your most comfortable shoes on...and a knapsack...it's a walking trail...first discovered by Indians who inhabited the area...we come to a small bridge over a brook...as you approach the bridge you notice the water rushing over the rocks...the bridge is very strong...very sturdily-constructed...you put your elbows on the railing and look down at the water below...watching the spray of foam as the water rushes by...fascinating...ever changing...soothing...the sun is coming in...it creates a rainbow across the stream...the colors are magnificent...the sun passes behind a cloud and you look at your watch and realize it's time to walk on...

"You walk past the trees...to a meadow...in the meadow there are flowers in bloom...butterflies flutter about...there's a wonderful smell in the air... walking ahead you approach a butterfly...it slowly moves off, and you follow it...to woods...

"This is not a forest, but you're immediately surprised to discover how pleasant it is...big shafts of light coming down...they cast incredible shadows...a chipmunk scurries off...you see a rabbit by a tree stump in the distance...he's nibbling on something...birds are chirping everywhere...as you come out of the woods, the trail divides...you take the one around the mountain to the big meadow...in winter, it's a ski slope...you soon come out at the top of the mountain, to the meadow...

"There's a stand of trees with a park bench...you put your knapsack down and take a seat on the bench...you have your lunch...observing the lake off in the distance...the sail boats...beyond, you see farms, patchworks of land, and another mountain range...you eat your lunch a bit at a time...you can hear the birds singing in the trees...as you look up, clouds are moving across the mountain range...

"Now you've finished your lunch. And maybe it's a combination of the walk and eating, but you feel yourself getting sleepy, and your head falls down gently on the back of the bench...and now you're looking up at the clouds...the wind is blowing the clouds...but your head is getting heavy and your eyelids are heavy, and you fall asleep...and in this comfortable sleep, you hear me and welcome the things that I say to you for your good..."

You should now apply the appropriate conditioning statement:

Smoking Conditioning

"I'm happy to tell you that from this moment on, you'll never need to smoke again in your entire life...you cannot be bothered to smoke...It doesn't matter now in what way you formerly smoked...if you smoked when you were driving...or after you ate...when you were on the phone...when you woke up...while you were reading...or at any time, that no longer applies...

"You see, instead of the habit of smoking, you now have the good habit of not smoking...of a calmness and self-control whenever and wherever you need it...it doesn't matter who offers you a cigarette or blows smoke in your face...you will not feel tempted or threatened, and you'll respond with something like, 'No thank you, I don't smoke anymore,' demonstrating that you now have control of your mind to make the decision and the will-power to carry it through...

"With each cigarette you no longer smoke, you're more and more reinforced in your new habit not to smoke...Also, there will be no substitution of any other habit on the physical level...you will not substitute eating for smoking...In fact, it is your desire to maintain your weight, or if you wish to lose weight, you'll be able to do so even now...now that you've stopped your smoking...

"The same new-found willpower you have acquired in no longer wanting to smoke is there for you in dieting and proper eating...You'll enjoy greater health in ways you may not expect to find...In a few days, your blood will clear and the effects of nicotine will be mainly gone...over a period of weeks and even months, the tars in your lungs will gradually diminish and leave your body...you will enjoy an energy level of unbelievable proportion...

"This is true because you will no longer be inhaling carbon monoxide from cigarettes. That carbon monoxide has been displacing oxygen in your blood...oxygen that should be finding its way to the far reaches of your body...instead, you have been deprived...deprived of oxygen, and instead, circulating poisons...but now, your body will be carrying rich, plentiful oxygen to the far reaches of your body...and your energy level will surge...you'll notice it in only a few days...

"You can use this new energy for many things...plan on doing extra things in business...family...sports...hobbies...in enjoying your life...in increased good health...

"It doesn't matter if, in the past, you had stopped smoking and started again...even repeatedly...no triggers, no emotions, no carelessness, or irresponsible decision-making will ever be a part of, or instrumental in, your returning to smoking...I'm happy to tell you that you'll never have to smoke again in your entire life...and each minute, hour, day, week, month, and year that passes, reinforces this wonderful habit you have NOT to smoke."

Dieting Conditioning

"I'm pleased to let you know that from now on, you'll diet beautifully...losing weight easily...down to your goal weight...where you will stay...You will enjoy sticking to your diet devotedly...Your diet is an excellent diet...you'll believe in it...you'll embrace it...you'll follow it...and you'll benefit from it...

"You'll not make exceptions in violation of the diet...you'll only substitute foods that are the nutritional equivalent...you'll diet in beautiful calmness, and patience, and pleasantness, and gentle firmness of purpose and resolve...

"Your stomach will be full and satisfied between meals and after your last meal of the day...when the time comes to eat, you will have a normal appetite for the proper amount of the right foods for that meal...Having eaten, your stomach, again, becomes full and satisfied until the next meal...or the following morning...

"You'll be most proud and happy with each half-pound you lose...you'll weigh yourself a few times a week rather than every day, and you'll enjoy the trend as you lose the weight...You'll find evidences of better health in many ways as your weight loss continues...

"You'll enjoy added strength, simply from less weight...You'll enjoy added health because you're eating healthy foods in a healthy way...

"You will exercise or engage in sports of your choice somewhere during your weight loss...It is important to keep skin and muscle firm when you lose weight...enjoy the thrill of having your body gradually matching your new slender image of yourself...

"You will stick to your diet and reach your goal weight in great happiness and health...if a plateau occurs where you're dieting honestly and not losing weight, don't be concerned...persist...in a week or a few days more weight will come off...the plateau was just time needed for your body to reshape itself...

"It doesn't matter if you eat out or at home...you'll only eat foods permitted on your diet...no one can force you or trick you into breaking your diet...because you are happy and devoted to it...no temptation...no emotions...no threats of any kind will change you in your resolve...you have a goal in weight and size and you have wonderful determination to reach your goal...

"I'm happy to tell you that you'll never overeat again in your entire life...and each minute, hour, day, week, month, and year that passes, reinforces this wonderful habit you have NOT to overeat."

Drinking Conditioning

"I'm happy to tell you that you'll never drink again in your life...from now on you can't be bothered drinking...it doesn't matter what you drank...in what

amount...where...or when...or how...you are devoted to never drinking again...and proud of each passing sober day...

"You owe NO allegiance to your drinking buddies...you only owe allegiance to yourself...your own health...and your own long life...

"You are now magnificently reclaiming yourself...Instead of the bad habit of drinking...and you know we mean alcoholic drink...you now have the new habit...the good habit of not drinking...and calmness and self-control...as you need it in life...

"If you visit your drinking friends, you'll have water or a soft drink...and you know that the other people with you won't care what you have...as long as they have what they want...

"They can offer you alcohol, but you insist on your soft drink or water...Very quickly...that is in a few days...you'll feel healthier...in body and mind...In a few weeks, you'll find that your memory of your drinking days is seldom considered...you'll also find that gradually you'll acquire new circles of friends...a beautiful closeness to your family...and greater success in business, hobbies, sports, and life...

"I congratulate you...you'll never drink again in all your life...and each minute, hour, day, week, month, and year that passes, reinforces this wonderful habit you have NOT to drink."

Pain Control Conditioning

Dealing with pain control is a much more complicated subject than, say, smoking or dieting. Pain can be a sprained ankle, childbirth, surgery, or the pain from a terminal illness.

One hundred years ago, large-scale major surgery, especially amputations, were performed without drugs or medicines, only hypnosis as an anesthesia.

Pain control can be an *analgesia*, to relieve chronic or episodic pain, or an *anesthesia*, to numb an area of the body, as you would in preparation of some medical procedure, such as dental surgery. Let's look at one script for anesthesia, followed by one for analgesia.

This first technique is called *glove anesthesia*. Here, the subject thinks of a past experience of having a hand or limb "go to sleep," or become numb, and then "transfers" that feeling to the affected area.

"I want you to imagine, if you will, that I have placed a large bucket of ice water next to your right hand...picture a large stainless steel bucket filled with ice and water,...the water is very cold...extremely cold...but very inviting...it's cool...inviting and cool...as you place your RIGHT arm into the water, it feels very cool and soothing...the water is so cold and soothing that you begin to notice that the coldness is numbing your hand...your hand is becoming numb...losing all sensation...it is growing more numb...the cold water feels very good...you are losing feeling in your right hand...it is as though

there is an absence of feeling in your hand...you know it's there, but you have no feeling in your hand...you have become unaware of any feeling in your right hand...

"I want you to imagine removing your hand from this bucket...and placing it on (the affected area, i.e., your right cheek, in preparation for dental surgery)...and feel the coldness...the power of your hand transferring its properties to the right side of your face...you will begin to experience the right side of your mouth becoming numb...as though you are unaware of any feeling in this region of your face...and when you say, 'Now,' any feelings or sensations will be gone in the right side of your face...and when you want the feelings to return, you will place your LEFT hand on the area, and the warmth of your hand will bring back the feelings you had before...

"I will count to five, and as I do, your (affected area) will grow completely numb, void of any feelings...one...growing numb...two...feel the coldness being absorbed in...three...numb, more numb...four...losing all sensation...five...totally numb..."

Now here's one for analgesia.

"I'm happy to tell you that from this moment on, you'll never need to feel unwanted pain again in your entire life...you know that you have the power within you to make this happen...

"I want you to think of time...that for each of us, there is a personal time, one not dependent on time pieces...this kind of time may be slower or faster than real time, but it's your personal time....you have experienced it many times...think back to all the times you were having so much fun, doing whatever it was that you were doing, that you lost track of time...that it seemed that hardly any time had passed, yet several hours had gone buy...Or, how about the times you were anxiously awaiting something...you wanted to open a present sitting in front of you, but you had to wait, what seemed like hours...but it was only minutes...

"We will use this ability of experiencing events in a personal time...the next time you have pain, no matter what the duration actually is by the clock, you will experience it as shorter...and thereafter, you will experience in your own personal time the duration of each pain as less and less...and again using your personal time, the time between pains will grow progressively longer...There will come a time when, in your personal time, each pain will be momentary...like a flash...and there will be an eternity of time between their occurrences...Only the pain will be affected by your personal time...all other events will match clock time, except when you want to enjoy something longer."

One thing to remember when dealing with pain: pain is the body's way of warning us of some internal problem or ailment we need to address. The long-term treatment of the root cause of the pain is always the best route. But, where no traditional treatment exists, such as a terminal illness, then hypnosis can be very helpful in relieving or eliminating the pain symptoms.

The Awakening Process

To follow the conditioning:

"I know that the benefit I get from this experience is a positive, healthy experience, and any time I wish to enter this state of ease again, all I need to do is relax in a comfortable position, take several deep breaths, and imagine myself on a wonderful adventure to my special place. Whenever I take several deep breaths and imagine this place, I will notice that I can quickly and easily return to the deep level of relaxation and comfort...

"You will now awaken yourself from this nap by counting backwards from four...and by the time I say 'one' and 'AWAKE,' you will be fully, fully, fully, totally, totally awake...FOUR...you're starting to WAKE...THREE...you're awakening slowly...TWO...you're almost totally awake...FOUR... AWAKE!...you are wide awake and feeling great!"

Self Hypnosis: The Short Version

Here's a similar self-hypnosis technique, only much shorter. As you become more adept at entering the trance state, you may want to try this shorter version. In a relaxed position, lying on a sofa, bed, or carpeted floor:

"Close your eyes...take a deep breath and hold it...let it out, and feel a sense of relaxation coming in as the air is expelled. Nothing harmful can happen to you...you are safe....just let whatever you find happening to you, happen... even if it is not what you expected...just let it occur...listen only to my voice and all that I describe...

"Picture, if you will, a still, calm pond...it's a beautiful pond surrounded by trees...and silence everywhere...the sun is warm, like in the early morning at sunrise, or in the evening at sunset...its warmth radiate through your body...

"Picture a drop of water falling into the pond...as it strikes the still, placid surface, it sends out ripples...as the ring of the first ripple spreads, a second one forms within it...then a third...and they come faster...ripples in ripples in ripples...a series of concentric circles...

"Feel the ripples of relaxation spreading out from your eyes...across the muscles of your forehead...down your face...lips...chin...Feel the spreading waves of relaxation in your neck...your shoulders...your back...your chest...your stomach...your arms...your fingers...your legs...your toes...

"Imagine yourself floating...drifting...gliding...on the still water...on a raft...peacefully drifting on a gentle current...moving ever so slowly....floating and moving without a care in the world...

"Visualize a leaf, a leaf fallen from a tree on a hill above floating down the calm river...you move gently along side the leaf...while you watch the leaf, mentally count backwards from 25 to one...slowly with each count, imagine the leaf drifting toward a quiet cove, a place where you are all alone...with no one to bother you...

"As the leaf and your counting slowly flow downstream, feel your muscles releasing stress and pressure...feel your whole body in a wave of relaxation...ping!...as ripples of waves of stress ungulate out...ripple after ripple...ping!...ripple after ripple...until you are in a total, complete, utter state of relaxation...25...24...floating...

23...22...drifting...21...20...slowly drifting...19...18...17...floating...16...15...14...13... 12...slowing floating...11...10...nine...eight...seven... ah, so relaxed...six...five... drifting...four...three...floating...two...one...

"Now that you are familiar with the state of realization you find yourself in, it will be easier and easier to enter more and more quickly this relaxed state whenever you wish to do so in the future...And in this wonderful state of relaxation you find yourself in, you hear me and welcome the things that I say to you for your good..."

At this point you add whatever conditioning statement applies. After the conditioning statement, finish with, *"I am going to count backwards from three, and at 'one' you will open your eyes and be fully alert, feeling refreshed and renewed, and your usual sensations and control will have returned. Now, 'three'...take a deep breath...'two'...let it out...'ONE!' ...fully alert, feeling great!"*

Rapid Self-Hypnosis Conditioning Statements:

CONDITIONING STATEMENT FOR SMOKING

"In my wonderful calmness and happiness and self-control, I will no longer smoke for the rest of my life." Repeat this statement three times in a row.

CONDITIONING STATEMENT FOR DIETING

"In my wonderful calmness and happiness and self-control, I am dieting beautifully and losing weight easily down to my goal weight, where I will stay." Repeat this statement three times in a row.

CONDITIONING STATEMENT FOR DRINKING

"In my wonderful calmness and happiness and self-control, I will no longer drink for the rest of my life." Repeat this statement three times in a row.

CONDITIONING STATEMENT FOR PROCRASTINATORS

"In my wonderful calmness and happiness and self-control, I now know what must be done, so I'll do first things first, promptly, fully, pleasantly, and skillfully." Repeat this statement three times in a row.

CONDITIONING STATEMENT FOR GOOD STUDY HABITS

"In my wonderful calmness and happiness and self-control, I will study with complete attention, fully concentrating, understanding and remembering" Repeat this statement three times in a row.

CONDITIONING STATEMENT FOR FEAR OF FLYING

"As I approach flying and as I fly, I do so in wonderful calmness and happiness and self-control." Repeat this statement three times in a row.

CONDITIONING STATEMENT FOR STRESS RELIEF

"As I lay here in the warmth and comfort of my surroundings, I watch the leaves falling from the trees...and as those leaves fall, they remind me of how I can let go of old problems and worries in my life...and let them fall away from me...just as old leaves fall from trees to make room for new growth and new changes." Repeat this statement three times in a row.

The Five Rules of Self Hypnosis

1. PRACTICE MAKES PERFECT. Each time you practice self-hypnosis, you reinforce the image and memory of the feeling of relaxation. Eventually, just bringing up the image or memory becomes your posthypnotic cue to produce the relaxing feeling.

2. MOTIVATION IS KEY. You have to *want* to change, before change will happen.

3. USE AS MANY SENSES AS YOU CAN. Try to employ all your senses. Visualize a scene, add plenty of color and detail. A mental image is worth a thousand words. Try to hear as many sounds as possible, and experience the aroma, texture, and taste, too.

4. ESTABLISH A GOAL AND WORK TOWARDS IT. You need to decide what goals you're trying to achieve with self-hypnosis, make them clear and achievable, and stick with it until you succeed.

5. SELF-HYPNOSIS IS A WAY OF LIFE. Self-hypnosis is not a pill you take once. It is a life-style you adapt to your daily schedule. It should be something to enjoy and look forward to.

Chapter

Odds & Ends

Harnessing the power of the mind

W hy do some people succeed in everything they do, while others are cast into lives of mediocrity? Why does one sibling go on to achieve fame and fortune, while the other ends up leading a life of crime and despair? Why do certain people seemingly possess an uncanny ability to make all the right choices, while others stumble from one problem to the next?

The Power Of The Mind

As you have found from reading this book, *a belief that one holds in the mind, consciously or subconsciously, once accepted, will be acted upon by our physical and mental being.* Think positively, and positive things will happen. Think negatively, and you'll be doomed to succeed -- at failing.

Does that mean if you think positively that everything you set out to do will automatically succeed? Absolutely not. It simply means that on the path to success, you won't let the minor annoyances stop your journey. It's not that successful people don't have problems. They do. They don't harp on them. They harp on what is right in what they're doing.

Underachievers and failures tend to focus on the bad. Fifty things in their day could be perfect, but, let one thing go wrong, and BAM! their whole day is lousy, everyone is out to get them, they have no "luck," and on and on.

Why do some athletes under stress, say, for instance, at the Olympic games, break all world records, while others expected to do so well, fail? The power of the mind. They psyche themselves. Some psyche themselves into believing that can win, against all odds. Some psyche themselves out of winning.

This process of conditioning your mind, of reinforcing beliefs, is a form of self-hypnosis. And we do it everyday. From the moment to wake up until we fall asleep. Ever wake up in the morning and look over at the clock, it's 6:00am, but you say to yourself, "Boy, I'm still tired. Maybe I should sleep in for another ten minutes"? So you do. And you *still* wake up tired. Then one day, there's something you *want* to wake up for. At 6:00am you leap out of bed.

Our beliefs about ourselves, or ability to shape our own destiny, our power to achieve life goals, is in our hands. All we need to do is use it.

Five Pathways To Greatness

Here are five pathways you can use to impel your mind into helping you reach your life goals.

1. USE YOUR WHOLE BRAIN

You can't achieve your maximum potential if you don't use your whole brain: the left brain *and* the right brain. Plan with the left brain and execute with the right brain.

The left side, or left hemisphere of your brain is where your knowledge lies. It is the library of all your experiences, analysis, and observations. This storehouse of information is *knowledge*, as opposed to *intelligence*. You can have vast knowledge, but not succeed in life. Intelligence is the ability to utilize knowledge for gain. There are homeless people with MBAs. There are millionaires who never finished grade school.

What puts that knowledge to practical use is our right brain, where our sensitivity and emotions reside. The right brain is what allows us to see beyond the facts, to push beyond the traditional boundaries, past the obvious, to new possibilities, new horizons, where success awaits those with patience and determination ("thinking outside the box").

Most successful businesses were started by people who, if they listened to convention wisdom, would have never been so foolhardy as to try what they tried. Sure, they did their homework. But when the time came to commit to their "dream," they chose instinct over logic.

But, *because* they did, they succeeded. Fred Smith challenged the U.S. Postal Service to create Federal Express. Bill McGowen challenged AT&T to create MCI Communications (now part of WorldCom, a company created by another equally successful entrepreneur, Bernie Ebbers. Everyone said the McDonald brothers couldn't make money selling 15 cent hamburgers. They proved the skeptics wrong. But they couldn't see beyond the potential of a few stores. It took Ray Kroc to envision the McDonalds of today, with fast food locations around the world. Bill Gates, Michael Dell, Dave Thomas, Sam Walton, Leslie Wexner (the Limited), and Barry Diller are but a handful of examples of other modern-day heroes who made their business dreams a reality.

Be willing to balance the left and right brain; to not be rigid, but not be too loose; to value facts, but be willing to "test the envelope".

2. THINK POSITIVE THOUGHTS, IMAGINE SUCCESS

What else did Fred Smith, Bill McGowen and Ray Kroc share in common? The drive to succeed, the singular vision of a company that would make it big. They saw their success from day one.

Even when things weren't going their way, they still believed. Because in each case, the ride to the top was a bumpy one. Their ventures could have failed, many times. But they didn't.

These people were able to look past the numbers, past the quantifiable data, to play their hunches, to use their right brain, too. They each had a game plan, they each had a strategy, but when the situation called for it, they were willing to side step it, to move outside the routine and linear thinking of most people. While they remained closed minded to the idea of failure, they were always open-minded to ideas.

The lesson to be learned here is to believe in your dream and don't ever let anyone or anything shake that ideal.

3. RELAX YOUR BRAIN

By studying the brain waves of people sleeping, scientists have discovered that the mind moves in cycles, each cycle lasting some 90 minutes, continuously, twenty-four hours a day. Our attention span, alpha waves, hunger, and performance levels can all vary based on where the mind is.

So what this tells us is that we have a natural span of attention, where we are most productive, just as we have a period where our alpha waves are highest, and therefore we are able to enjoy vivid daydreams.

Successful people know, consciously or not, how to pace themselves to take advantage of their mind cycles. They know when to work hard, and when to relax. They know when to think of solutions, and they know when to push ahead.

Want an example of this is practice? Ever have a problem that was bothering you, so you went out and did something physical, like jog, chop wood, or clean the house? And as you started to relax and get into the activity, the answer to your problem popped into your head? You were listening to your mind cycles. You relaxed your body and your mind, and allowed the mind to daydream (move into the subconscious mind) where the answer was.

The lesson to be learned here is to succeed, you must learn to relax your mind so you can think clearly.

4. SET SUCCESS GOALS

Goals give purpose and meaning to life. We all set "big" goals: we want to get married, we want a house, a car, three children, lots of money. What you need to do is set a lot of "little" goals.

Instead of saying, "My new business has to be a huge success, or else," say, "This week I want to achieve these small goals." Maybe it's the number of new prospective accounts you call on. Or how many new solutions you can think of for the same problem. Success breeds success. Small successes lead to bigger successes. Pin all your hopes on one big goal, and two things happen: First, it may be a long time before you achieve this objective, and you may lose your will to push on; and two, you can't enjoy all the little pleasures that happen along the way.

The moral is to think globally (big picture), but act locally (small picture). You'll achieve more, and be a happier person.

5. FAILURE IS ONLY FOR USERS

Finally, always remember that failure is only a mental state. When you realize that there is no such thing as failure, *except the failure not to try,* then you can only succeed.

Some Final Words Of Wisdom

Hypnosis can be a fun hobby. But it has a serious side, too. We're dealing with people's minds, and when you do that, you need to be conscious of the longer-term effects that can happen.

For instance, when you show someone glove anesthesia to remove pain, don't forget that the pain is there for a reason. Pain and fatigue are signals from our body, ways of attracting our attention to a problem. To mask or remove these symptoms may exacerbate a situation that needs real and immediate medical attention.

Speaking of "medical," I'd like to point out the obvious. This book is not meant to be a short course in how to be a professional hypnotist, able to cure people of all their problems. It will not make you a doctor or give you the background needed to diagnosis and treat patients.

Finally, be careful in choosing subjects. Some people, because of their mental state, should *not* to hypnotized, at least not by an amateur hypnotist. It may cause them problems and it may cause you problems. Always remember that the power of the mind is not a play-toy. Respect its power. Unexpected circumstances, when you're working with something as mysterious as the human brain, can happen, unexpected circumstances beyond your ability to cope with the problem. If you find yourself with a subject who exhibits any strange behavior, break off the session immediately. You are not a trained medical professional. You don't want to harm the person, or find yourself embroiled in any legal difficulties.

In Conclusion

No one knows what the limits are of the human mind. There's still a lot we have yet to discover about how our brain works and what we can do to maximize our mind's potential.

Emerson said it best. *"The gates of thought — how slow and late they discover themselves! Yet when they appear, we see that they were always there, always open".*

You now have the knowledge to hypnotize people. You know its "secrets." Now practice, practice, practice. And then go out and have *fun* with it.

Hypnotism offers great challenge, reward, and self-fulfillment. I wish you the best of luck and success with your new-found skills!

Bibliography

Adams, Paul T., *The New Self-Hypnosis.* North Hollywood, California: Wilshire Book Company, 1967.

Alman, Brian M. Ph.D., Lambrou, P. Ph.D.,*Self-Hypnosis, The Complete Manual For Health and Self-Change.* New York: Brunner/Mazel, 1985.

Baker, Robert A., *They Call It Hypnosis,* Buffalo, New York: Prometheus Book, 1990.

Cook, Wm. Wesley, *Practical Lessons in Hypnotism.* New York: Willey Book Company, 1927.

Edmonston, William E., Jr., *The Induction of Hypnosis,* New York: John Wiley & Sons, 1986.

Furst, Arnold,*Rapid Induction Hypnosis And Self Hypnosis.* Alhambra, California: Borden Publishing, 1982.

Kelly, Sean F. Ph.D., Kelly, Ried J., *Hypnosis: Understanding How It Can Work For You,* Reading, Massachusetts: Addison Wesley, 1985.

Kreskin, *Secrets of the Amazing Kreskin,* Buffalo, New York: Prometheus Book, 1991.

Leonidas, Professor (pseud.), *Secrets of Stage Hypnotism,* Hollywood, CA: Newcastle Publishing, 1975.

McGill, Ormond, *The Encyclopedia of Genuine Stage Hypnotism,* Colon, Michigan: Abbott's Magic Novelty Co., 1947.

McGill, Ormond, *The Art of Stage Hypnotism,* Alhambra, California: Borden Publishing, 1975.

Ousby, William J., *The Theory and Practice of Hypnotism,* Northamptonshire, England: Thorsons Publishers Limited, 1990.

Pilos, Lee, *Beyond Hypnosis,* San Francisco, CA: Omega Press, 1990.

Pratt, George J. Jr., Ph.D., Wood, Dennis P. Ph.D., Alman, Brian M. Ph.D., *A Clinical Hypnosis Primer,* La Jolla, California: Psychology & Consulting Associates Press, 1984.

Weitzenhoffer, Andre M., *The Practice of Hypnotism, Volume One & Volume Two,* New York: John Wiley & Sons, 1989.

About The Author

Professor Svengali shortly after arriving in Paris (circa 1978)

Professor Svengali (Sir Reginald "Reggie" Barrister, III) is a world-renown author and lecturer. Professor Svengali was graduated from London University in 1961 with a BA in Parapsychology. After a 14-year stint in the United Nations as Chief Medical Advisor to the Committee on Mental Health in Underdeveloped Countries, he taught Clinical Hypnosis at Cambridge.

Actually, there is no Professor Svengali. That's my stage name. I'm David Geliebter. I live in New Jersey with my wife and two children. This isn't even my picture. It's from a royalty-free stock photography CD I bought for $49.95. I'm a graduate of the American School of Hypnosis and have practiced stage hypnosis for the last several years. My other hobbies include magic and martial arts.

Notes

Notes

Notes

Notes